Jackie, Oy!

Jackie, Oy!

JACKIE MASON FROM BIRTH TO REBIRTH

by
Jackie Mason
with Ken Gross

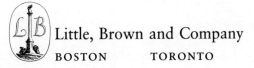
Little, Brown and Company

BOSTON   TORONTO   LONDON

FIRST EDITION

Library of Congress Catalog Card Number 88-13415

10 9 8 7 6 5 4 3 2 1

Published simultaneously in Canada
by Little, Brown & Company (Canada) Limited
PRINTED IN THE UNITED STATES OF AMERICA

To my father
— Jackie Mason

*To Fredrica Friedman, who took us
down the yellow-slip road*
— Ken Gross

Jackie, Oy!

CHAPTER ONE

The Fickle Finger

Timing. It's very easy to screw up timing. Like in a joke. Here's a good example:

"The most important thing in the world is not money, because money does not make you happy. I know a guy who lives in a house without a sink, without water, without a ceiling. He has nothing. But he's happy. Do you know why? . . . *He's stupid!*"

That's a joke that depends on exact timing. If you say it a fraction of a second too fast, where the buildup is not accentuated with enough emotion or intensity or expressiveness and believability, it won't work. Has to be exact. Like, if I said:

"I know a guy who lives in a house without a sink, without water, without a ceiling, he has nothing, but he's happy. You know why? He's stupid!"

Now if you say it like that, if you give it just a half a second beat instead of a full second, you'll only get one-tenth the laugh. If you give an audience an opportunity to absorb the significance of the point —

and wait an extra second or two — all of a sudden, the same joke gets a scream.

Timing is everything.

What Jackie Mason did not understand on that crucial morning of October 18, 1964, was that his timing — that subtle, sensuous universal beat that marks the difference between stardom and all other show-business ranks — was still years off. He awoke that Sunday as he awoke every day of his adult life: expecting to be proclaimed a major star. When it didn't happen, he could never understand why. He had talent, youth, ambition. And he believed in himself. Maybe no one else believed in him, but he had enough faith for everyone — a kind of blind, mystical conviction — the sort of thing that he was never quite able to muster for his earlier vocation: religion. Despite all the days of relative obscurity, Jackie never doubted his comic destiny.

The apartment in which he awoke did not look like the headquarters of a star. It was as stark and devoid of human comforts as a cell. There were no paintings on the walls. There were no flowers on the table. The single window looked out upon the bare brick face of yet another Manhattan apartment building. Jackie Mason didn't mind. He didn't take it personally. He might live like a monk, but it was only temporary. He had more urgent business than fancy decorating schemes. He was busy waiting to become a star. By now, it should have happened. There had been enough opportunities. He was making regular guest appearances on "The Ed Sullivan Show" as well as "The Perry Como Show" and "The Dean Martin Show," "The Gary Moore

*Show." In addition to appearing every few weeks on
the variety shows, Jackie was pulling down as much as
$10,000 a week in nightclubs.*

*And yet he remained stuck in that secondary B orbit
of minor fame, one step below a household name. He
was not Milton Berle or Buddy Hackett or Lenny Bruce
or even Alan King. He made the television appearances, but they seemed to leave no lasting impression.
He convulsed the audiences with his jokes, but the laughs
were there and then they were gone; they left only a
shadow, not fame. Somehow, stardom — real, instant-
recognition superstardom — remained just out of his
reach.*

*"Tell me," he would beseech members of the public,
pulling them aside at every opportunity, "honestly, do
you think I'm a star?" In supermarkets and coffee shops,
walking on the street, he would stop strangers and put
them through the winger. "What do you think I should
do to become a smash hit?" he would implore. The
baffled civilians would blurt out wild guesses — "Get
your own show!" "You're already a star in my book!" —
but there was no good answer to the question of sur-
passing importance to Jackie Mason: Why isn't Jackie
Mason a big superstar?*

I wouldn't say it was making me crazy. But I
thought about it. I can't deny that I thought about
it. And it was a puzzle. I knew that I was a fantastic
smash hit with the public. I knew that if I got in
front of an audience, there was no audience I couldn't
destroy. And yet, I felt I was not going anywhere. I
was busy, but I wasn't causing a traffic jam. I couldn't
find an answer. It was like having something on the

tip of your tongue but you can't think of it. Come to think of it, this was making me a little crazy.

What he had to do, he thought, was to find some-thing to get the full attention of the American public. It would take more than one killer routine, one mo-ment that they couldn't ignore. It would take ... something ... he didn't know what. He knew that it was right there, right in front of his eyes, like one of those moral, philosophical riddles that they tried to blind you with in Hebrew school, but he couldn't see it.

As soon as he opened his eyes in the morning, the former rabbi, who had long since exchanged his high spiritual calling to join the secular order of stand-up comedians, began to look for material that would con-vince everyone else that he was who he thought he was.

As usual, he turned to the mundane details around him. The material was the material of everyday life:

Life was ridiculous enough without much inven-tion. You didn't have to look too far for comedy material. For instance, I had a routine about my new luxury apartment: "I moved into a new apartment. I had to give the landlord three hundred dollars for the first month's rent, three hundred dollars for the last month's rent, and three hundred dollars for se-curity. Does this make sense? I give this man nine hundred dollars and he wants references from me. I should get references from him. Am I going to steal his apartment? Where would I hide it?"

Jackie placed the tape recorder on a plain table and worked and reworked the material. As he listened, his

hand automatically moved to the top of his head, where
he once wore his yarmulke. He played with the hair on
the dome of his head. An absentminded tic, perhaps.
Or, looked on in a certain way, it could be viewed as
a man hedging his bet, substituting his hand for the
forsaken skullcap. One way or another, his head was
still covered in respect.

Look how he makes something out of nothing. Since
when is it a crime to touch your head? Touching other
things, maybe, but an innocent gesture becomes a
major criminal act in the hands of an amateur ana-
lyst. Look, you have to do something with your hands
when you talk, am I right? You can't just sit there
like a putz. Maybe you can, but I can't. So, it happens, that I touch my head. It happens — by pure
coincidence — that it is the same spot where I wore
a yarmulke. Where would I wear a yarmulke, on my
nose? And if I played with my nose, would this man
find great spiritual meaning in that, or would I be a
slob? What's the big mystery? If you wear something, a piece of fabric, anything, on your head for
the first ten, fifteen years of your life, you get used
to something being there. Doesn't that make sense?
Or, maybe it's even something very simple. Maybe
your head is cold. But to read deep, phony psycho-
logical significance into the fact that I touch my head,
that maybe I'm searching for a lost God, that I could
be expressing some hidden spiritual need, this is the
product of a sick mind. Am I making myself clear?

On the Sunday of the Sullivan show, Jackie fiddled
with his head and played the tape recorder. The rou-

tines had to be word perfect, and timed down to the second. It was one thing to stand up in a nightclub where you had an hour onstage; you could run over the allotted time, as much as fifteen minutes. The next act was late, was all. But on television, time was doled out like heartbeats. A man with a stopwatch stood off-camera, ready to lop off your best punch line if you trespassed into somebody else's career. And this was not some local show where you could fail safely. Ed Sullivan had a popular weekly variety show and Jackie would be talking to forty million people. Any appearance could be the crucial one, the one that broke through that hard crust of resistance and made him the toast of the town. Jackie pressed the "record" button and spoke as he would speak to his national audience about his apartment building:

"They give you things in these new apartments that mean nothing. Music in the elevator. A great luxury. What would a normal person care if he got music in the elevator or not? I live on the first floor; how much music can I hear by the time I get there? The guy on the twenty-eighth floor, let him pay for it. I'm running a concert for a guy I don't even know. I wanna get my money's worth, so you know what I do now? Every night I come home two hours early, I go up and down, I listen. There was a time I took a girl to a nightclub. No more. I take her to the elevator. I bring in a couple of drinks with hors d'oeuvres, I bring a friend with a tuxedo. She thinks she's having a good time. Things that they give you! Like a walk-in closet. Do you wanna go for a walk in the closet?

When was the last time you went to the closet to go for a walk?"

Perfect timing. Perfect delivery. Jackie was blessed with utter confidence in his own talent. He practiced until the parts of the monologue fit together flawlessly. In the most profound way, he understood humor. Which was also why he was so frustrated. There was no good reason why he was not a national sensation. There was, however, one bad reason. The self-styled critics who ran the business end of show business danced around, avoiding naming the reason. They said Jackie was "too regional." Or "too urban." Or that he had a "limited appeal." Sometimes they even used the word "ethnic." What they meant, and what they sometimes blurted out in frustration when Jackie refused to see their point, was that he was "too Jewish." That is, he spoke with a thick Yiddish accent.

The accent was pronounced, and it was very melodious, rising up and down the scales like a song, ending always in a prophetic upbeat question mark. There was text in the inflection. Yiddish was spoken in shrugs. But it was — according to the business managers and agents — a sound that conjured up the guttural Lower East Side of New York, the discord of immigrant pushcart peddlers, the coarse vulgarity of garment center tycoons. It was colorful, but they all agreed that it should be quarantined in the Catskill Mountains. In the Borscht Belt hotel lounges, the accent was like a beloved antique fragrance or an Old World portrait of ancestors wearing stiff collars and brittle smiles — things cherished but best enjoyed in private. In that setting, Jackie was funny. He was a smash. But you wouldn't put your grandfather on national television, they seemed to suggest. You wouldn't show the "goyim" your secret vulnerabilities. It was a jarring invitation to arouse anti-Semites. With that accent, Jackie might as well be wearing a yellow star on his sleeve.

You have to laugh. To the agents and managers I was too Jewish. To my family, I was not Jewish enough. My father was a pious religious fanatic who spent all day and all night buried in books, studying the Talmud, worrying and praying that his youngest son should forget this show-business craziness and become a good rabbi, which was, in his eyes, the only real job for a man. Everything else was a waste of time. These agents and managers, you know who they were, these agents and managers? Not escaped Nazis. They all had fathers who spoke like me. They were Jews.

Listen, said the managers and agents, lose the accent. Get a voice job. You're a young, hip guy. It'll take no time at all.

They even offered to pay for the lessons.

Jackie refused. He changed his name from Jacob Maza to Jackie Mason, but that was as far as he was willing to go. There was no shame in an accent, he declared. The shame was being ashamed. Besides, that same obstinate instinct that told him what was funny, told him that his accent was a crucial factor in his humor. He was not about to tamper with God-given talent.

Jackie read the morning newspapers with a ferocious appetite. He never read his morning prayers (when he was still reading his morning prayers) with the passion that he now read the newspapers. Look at this, he said out loud to the empty room. Look at this, the Chinese have the bomb! Just what we need. All the news was shock and life to Jackie Mason. And yet, he remained aloof. The only real risk was getting ink on his hands from the newspapers. He was, by nature, an observer. He stood apart and watched the world stumble through another twenty-four hours, commenting, criticizing to thin air. The whole idea of being a stand-up comedian was to do it from the protected sanctuary of a stage. He wasn't just wasting his breath on four empty walls. First he had to try out the reactions alone, like a singer practicing scales. Then he would work on the audience.

There wasn't much doing in today's newspaper. At least, not much that was funny. A new leader had re-placed Nikita Khrushchev in Russia; there was an election coming up in America and the campaign was in full swing. Barry Goldwater was deep into his futile attempt to unseat Lyndon Johnson for the presidency. That was feeble material for satire on tonight's Sullivan show, but you needed something topical.

I don't like political jokes. Some guy's in office for ten minutes and you invent a routine and then he doesn't get reelected and I'm out of business. Why should I take on a partner?

Uninspired, Jackie took a shower then went to his favorite haunt: a coffee shop. Manhattan was freckled with coffee shops — those urban anchorages that gave him the real feeling of warming himself at a hearth. He didn't mind the greasy counters and stale pastries and the impatience of the workers. It was all worth it, just to hear the talk. The coffee shops were like some expanded version of the family kitchen table and wherever he went — in New York or on the road — it was there that Jackie Mason felt at home. In the booths and around the counters he could overhear the earthy humor, the hard-won wisdom and the folk tales of America. There is also the unfiltered look at life through the eyes of the people who come and go over coffee. Not much happens that isn't chewed over across the counters. The news of the day is examined and digested in that plain light.

He could also bother people gently, asking them their opinions about world events. He was always curious about opinions. Opinions about the weather, about sports, about politics. On this Sunday in New York, there were a lot of opinions about the presidency. People were worried about Barry Goldwater and his so-called quick trigger. Lyndon Johnson might sound like some thick-witted redneck, but he was a Democrat and he spoke cautiously about war — not like this Goldwater with his knitted brows and defiant rhetoric about extremism in defense of liberty. Jackie thought maybe he should reconsider tonight's routine. Since it was on everyone's mind, maybe he should throw in a few quick jokes about the election. He sat in the coffee shop with his usual breakfast of a bagel and cream cheese and coffee and worked on a routine.

I would always try to sneak a routine into a conversation, to surprise people with the jokes. No matter what people were talking about, I'd pretend that

I was just running a part of a conversation. To make them seem incidental. If you ask someone, "Do you think this is funny?," I find that you set up a guard of self-conciousness. If a person is sitting there as a judge, he doesn't react the same way as when he's just hit with it. So you say a few things. And you watch the reaction: "The budget of this country was one hundred thirty-six billion dollars last year. Do you know what I gave them? Twelve dollars. Without my twelve dollars they can't get along? First spend the one hundred thirty-six billion, then, if you're twelve dollars short, give me a call." This went over big. This you could see was very good material.

The camera saw a short, wistful man in a business suit and a tie, a stitch over five feet four, with a glint of irreverence in his eyes. He stood on his mark, wearing half of a smile, which was about all he could manage. The laugh, when he made his jokes (which he appreciated as much as anyone), was also highly qualified. It came out like a cough, as if he had to restrain himself. The overall effect that Jackie Mason made was of a tightly bound intellectual who might, judging by the madness in his humor, spring out of control at any moment.

The dress rehearsal was always held at four in the afternoon at the CBS theater on Broadway. Ed Sullivan, a newspaper columnist who had become the host of the variety show, would come down from his fourth-floor suite of offices and monitor the routines from the wings.

I did the routine in the dress rehearsal and it was a big winner. Ed Sullivan came over to me and said hello, how are you. But we didn't say too much because he was by nature a very nervous man. Very tense. There was an atmosphere of great tension before an "Ed Sullivan Show" because his whole staff around him would be staring at him and he would be full of tension and pacing, looking very taxed and exacting. You could sense in him a kind of tension, an amount of anticipation, like his wife was going to have a baby. He looked like that before every show. And it rubbed off on his whole staff and he hardly talked. He looked tense and nervous, but he wasn't unpleasant. After the dress rehearsal, I would go to a coffee shop with my manager, Bobby Chartoff, who is now a big Hollywood producer, and my friend Bernie Weber. I didn't want to sit in the dressing room and get tense, like a fighter before a fight.

This is not the way everyone remembers it. The dress rehearsal, say some, was anything but smooth. President Lyndon Johnson was scheduled to tell the nation in person about the Chinese nuclear device and about the change in leadership in Moscow. Aleksei Kosygin had replaced Nikita Khrushchev, and like most Kremlin changes, it was sudden, unexpected, and a little frightening. If no one else, it made Ed Sullivan very nervous. Lyndon Johnson had decided to tell the nation right in the middle of his show. It was impossible to know whether Sullivan was nervous over world events or the disruption of his show.

In any case, Sullivan's son-in-law and producer, Bob Precht, approached Mason after the dress rehearsal. The political jokes have to go, he told Jackie. No jokes about how, with Lady Bird and Luci Bird and Linda Bird,

we had a government that was for the birds. Sullivan,
said Precht, did not want to pollute the political atmo-
sphere.

I don't remember this. I remember that Johnson
made an address. But I don't remember any problem
with jokes. I thought the dress rehearsal was great, I
thought that I was a sensation, I thought that Sullivan came over and complimented me and I don't remember any trouble.

By showtime, Jackie Mason felt the tingle of his own
nerves. You couldn't do what he did without some ef-
fect. But once he got on stage, once he had the audi-
ence laughing, he began to relax. Jackie Mason was on
just after Lyndon Johnson made his speech and Ed Sul-
livan was standing there in the studio, right behind the
camera, in full view of the audience, trying to signal
the comedian to tighten it up. He held up two fingers,
indicating the amount of time left for Jackie. Suddenly,
the audience that he had in the palm of his hands was
distracted by the off-camera antics of Sullivan.

The whole audience was watching his fingers instead of me. The example I always use is when a
busboy is walking around with a tray of dishes in
front of a speaker. Everybody watches the tray of
dishes. They forget that the guy is speaking. He could
be in the middle of the most powerful speech ever
delivered, making the most profound point of his life,
but let a busboy start walking with a tray and you'll
notice immediately how every eye starts to follow the
tray to see where he's going to land with the tray of

dishes. I saw, when he started to move his fingers and he was killing the laugh of my punch line, so to compensate for it, I started to make fun of his finger gestures, figuring this will make the people at home aware of why I just lost my laugh. So I started to ridicule his gestures by saying "Look at this, I'm telling jokes and he's showing me fingers. Nobody came to watch the fingers. If they came to watch the fingers, you would be here with fingers. How come I'm here with jokes? I'm here with jokes because nobody cares about a person standing, moving around fingers. If you got a finger for me, I got a finger for you."

All the time he was speaking, Jackie was flashing fingers. If you looked carefully, you would never find the one-finger salute. Technically, he never fired a shot. But fingers were flashed and the suggestion was plain. Jackie claims that it was all innocence. He swears that he had no idea that the upraised middle finger was an insult. He believes it, too. However, this is like a talented fan dancer claiming that sex has nothing to do with it.

By the time he came off the stage, Jackie Mason's career had taken a sudden turn for the worse. Ed Sullivan had, indeed, thrown off his timing. By more than two decades.

Why, in the course of a very short time, has Jackie Mason become one of the top comics of TV? Well, not long ago Mason was playing an engagement in Detroit. His manager explained to us that obviously Jackie couldn't get to New York City for mid-week rehearsals. . . . On Thursday of that week, Thanksgiving Day, our doorbell rang and there to my amazement was Jackie Mason. . . . When you have a performer who is that conscientious about his work, you have a performer who is marked for stardom.

In one of our TV shows, Jackie was trying to impress on me the fact that despite his accent, Mason once taught Sir Laurence Olivier how to speak English. "As a result," said Jackie, "today Olivier is one of the greatest dramatic stars in the world. . . ."

That illustrates the hilarious style that Mason has brought to the stage. Couple this type of humor with his manner of accenting his comedy with abrupt movements of his thumb and forefinger and you get a picture of him. . . . He is bright and brash and very funny. And he is a fine human being.

— Liner notes by Ed Sullivan
on Jackie's second comedy album

Jackie Mason was one of his favorite comedians, but the late Ed Sullivan was a mule. Things had to be done his way. Period. And he had a bad temper. If he suspected that a comedian was trying to slip something off-color past his censorious ear, he would fly into a rage. If, during the show, a performer deviated from the material he used before the preview audience — material approved and often dictated by Sullivan himself — that performer would be banished from his Sunday night program. When it came to his authority, Sullivan had very thin skin. And so the sight of Jackie Mason offering "a finger for you, a finger for you, a finger for you," and literally thumbing his nose at the camera, was unbearable. The great stone face of Ed Sullivan was not smiling when he approached Jackie Mason after the show on that night in 1964.

I had no intimation at all. I thought I was a hero because I got huge laughs. I thought that he loved it because I finished with such big laughs, I managed to make a difficult predicament, which was a negative situation where the audience didn't laugh because they were watching his fingers instead of me, and I managed to convert it into a big laugh. Ordinarily, you would say that he ruined my pacing and timing by popping in and making those gestures and I lost the audience from a couple of punch lines. But I was proud of myself because I accomplished a big thing, to have the presence of mind to do this and I thought he would be proud of me, because to me, it was innocent fun. I really thought he was coming over to congratulate me.

But he didn't. He looked at me with a venom and a hate like you never saw in your life and he said, "Who the fuck are you, you son-of-a-bitch, to make gestures like that at me?! You rotten bastard! I'll get even with you if it's the last thing I do! You'll never be on television again if I can help it! I'm going to see to it that you never work again in this business!"

Bobby Chartoff, Jackie Mason's manager, stood near the "wailing wall," where agents waited for verdicts during auditions, far in the background, witnessing the outburst, silent. All the witnesses stood far back — as far back as they could get. There was no point trying to intercede. The temper, like a storm, had to run its course. Once, Woody Allen was subjected to the same sort of abuse. Rather than confront Sullivan, rather than counterattack, Woody Allen had a different tactic. He tucked his tail between his legs and acted con-

trite. It worked. When the storm was over, it was Sullivan who was contrite. Woody Allen became a Sullivan favorite.

But this didn't look like a passing storm to the people watching from the wings. This looked like a killer rage. Ed Sullivan, nervous enough about a presidential address breaking into the middle of his live show, took Jackie's gestures as a double insult. Not only had the comedian flashed fingers at him — fingers which could only have one meaning — but he had used material about the government, which Sullivan had specifically forbidden. The jokes about the budget were, to Ed Sullivan, politics: a double act of insubordination.

Jackie's mouth opened and closed as he tried in vain to explain his position, to wiggle out of trouble, but Sullivan went further and deeper into his tirade.

At first I thought this was some kind of joke. Then I started to realize, "This man is serious," so I tried to answer, but he wouldn't let me. I was trying to say, "I didn't mean it that way, you got the wrong idea." I was desperately trying to get a word in edgewise and to make him realize that he was making a fantastic mistake, that he got the wrong impression, but he wouldn't let me talk. He kept screeching and screaming, "Who the fuck are you?!" and I said, "But that's not what I meant," and he said, "Who the hell do you think I am that you're gonna bullshit me, you rotten bastard, to tell me that's not what you meant?! Fucking lying bastard!" Cursing violently, screaming nothing but four-letter words, one on top of each other, and I said to myself, "It's a hopeless case to try to talk to this man."

Bob Precht says that he informed Jackie then and there that he was canceling his $45,000 contract for six appearances. Telegrams to that effect were going out to all the newspapers and wire services from Sullivan's headquarters at the studio on Broadway and 53rd Street. Jackie was in a state of shock. He didn't bother to change out of his show suit. He didn't even remove his stage makeup. He just grabbed his coat and left, trailing Chartoff and loyal friend Bernie Weber. They wandered the streets of Manhattan, trying to absorb the meaning of what had just taken place.

"It's okay," Chartoff kept saying.

"The best thing that could have happened," agreed Weber.

And all the while, Jackie Mason shook his head and pretended — even to himself — that it was a tempest in a teapot. It did not sink in that the finger he raised against Ed Sullivan would get stuck in the eye of the American public.

I didn't get too scared because I felt, in the back of my mind, I'll straighten it out with him one way or another because he'll realize that he made a grave mistake. Besides, I thought that I was pretty popular and the other shows will still grab me, so somehow, I was saying to myself, "If this man is that sick that he's blaming me for something that I never did, if he's insane, why should I let that bother me? What he's doing is nuts!"

What he also thought, the thing that he shamelessly calculated as he hurried out of the studio and into the night, was that this incident could be turned to his ad-

vantage. This could lead to publicity. And publicity, he was told again and again by Chartoff and Bernie Weber, is all to the good. This incident could be the big breakthrough. Such thoughts were not completely unreasonable in that desperately limp season of Jackie's career. He could not imagine that he could be ruined by something so playful — even if it did seem mischievous, maybe even of questionable taste for a man who once called himself rabbi.

I didn't think it was such a big deal. Until I got home. All we'd talked about was how vulgar Ed Sullivan was and how I was an innocent victim of his sick imagination. But when I walked in the door of my apartment, after leaving Bobby and Bernie, the phone was ringing. It was London. I was shocked. Some reporter from the London *Times.* The London *Times!* Can you believe this? They asked me what happened. And I repeated that it was a total misunderstanding and the reporter asked me why he canceled my contract. How should I know? The reporter asked me, Do you think you're gonna fight him? And I said absolutely, positively, I certainly will. Then I get a call from Tokyo and Paris and the Philippines and this is when I started to think that this is gonna be so great that maybe I'll become the biggest star in the world from this publicity. I called Bobby Chartoff and I said, "You know, we should really take advantage of this publicity because everybody wants to write a headline story." They all said that this is going to make the front page. I said, "You're actually going to tell this story?" because I said to myself, "A finger is worth such a story?" I couldn't imagine, I couldn't envision it. One little Jewish comedian, who is not even a major star, and just because he made a gesture that the boss of the show didn't like, he's fired. I couldn't imagine that this was of any major consequence, certainly not worthy of a headline. Maybe a gossip column or a back page. To think that this was of such immense importance in the annals of the world, that in the middle of the Vietnam war with President Johnson on television and the Chinese dropping a bomb — and the very next day the story of my finger wiped out the whole Vietnam war — I was the major headline for the next few days. I thought it was fantastic.

There were worried calls from all the members of his family — who were astonished by the commotion made by his appearance on the Sullivan show. Jackie reassured his brothers and sisters that he would not be hurt by being fired. They didn't understand show business, he said soothingly. Feuds are good business. Gets you free publicity.

The unsophisticated brothers and sisters — rabbis and housewives — who knew only what Jackie and their gut instincts told them about show business, were not reassured. Maybe even Jackie wasn't. Maybe they heard something in his voice, some low counterpoint of worry, which was the true reaction to the occasion.

Between calls from all over the world, Jackie telephoned Bobby Chartoff, who already had some intimation about the dimensions of the event. Phones were ringing. Reactions were solicited. Reporters were taking the temperature of the waters. Jackie and Bobby decided that they better meet at Downey's, a show-

business hangout at 45th Street on Eighth Avenue, and reassess what had happened.

Downey's was one of the old-style show-business restaurants where the waiters (unemployed actors, disappointed playwrights, one step away from show business themselves) knew everyone, knew every routine, and served show-business gossip and contempt along with the onion rolls. The trouble was that the waiters did not mention the incident, which was, in itself, disconcerting.

Jackie and Bobby were nervously waiting for the bulldog edition of the New York Times, *sitting at a table with untouched danish and cold coffee. They might have been waiting for X rays by the grim concern at their table. When the paper finally did appear, at 12:30 in the morning, it shattered the complacency of the evening. A full column in the* New York Times *about a show-business spat was no longer publicity. Jackie Mason and his manager felt the ground shift under their feet. It was impossible to tell whether this was good or bad now. But it was easy to tell that it was momentous.*

I thought it was nothing. I really did. And I was there.

By the next day, the full realization that there were unwelcome consequences to some kinds of publicity began to dawn on Jackie Mason. That Monday night, he was booked into the Town and Country, a popular nightclub in Brooklyn. There were less than a hundred people in the club that could seat more than ten times that many. Jackie Mason began his act with a joke. It was a joke that blew like an icy wind across the near-empty club: "Good evening tables and chairs."

I can't believe that I ever became conscious of the negative reaction. I couldn't pin down a moment. There was a kind of looking in the mirror at yourself every day; at what age did you find yourself aging? You look at your own face in the mirror and you never know when you started aging. It's a process that you can see if a guy comes back ten years later. But when you look at yourself every day, you really don't notice any changes. I really didn't see any specific change at any specific time. I just kept gauging myself, trying to become bigger and bigger, and I noticed that I wasn't getting bigger and bigger.

Well, I was always examining myself in that light. Before the Sullivan show I would hear, "Too Jewish." After the show, I would periodically hear that I'm too dirty.

Jackie Mason was not going to give up trying to become a major American superstar. He had gone through too much as it was. He had already brought forth a miracle, just getting this far.

CHAPTER TWO

Born in the U.S.A.

I'm not really curious about my ancestors. I don't want to save any family histories or pictures. I don't want to remember the exact date when I played a certain club because, to me, a perfect chronology is meaningless. Yesterday's news. I don't feel I'm gonna learn anything and I don't want to bore everyone else with a lot of pointless information. As far as the quest for a person's past, I believe that it's a sick kind of vanity that leads nowhere. Do I care that two hundred years ago I had a distant cousin who read a book? Does it have any significance whatsoever? All right, maybe if it's a dirty book, then we can assume the man was at least interesting. It could even explain all these ancestors. But as a general proposition, my own point of view is that it is meaningless. Maybe I want to know something about my father, maybe that has some importance. I could see a direct link between the generations. I could relate to that. But here's another thing: Now that I'm doing well who wants to find my ancestors? I'll find I have an

eighth or ninth cousin who has to be supported. I
support enough relatives now. Besides, the question
is, Does it really matter?

*And yet, all his disclaimers aside, it matters. In ways
we are not able to measure, it matters that Jackie Mason had sturdy ancestors who passed along things besides a familiar face in the mirror. No matter what he
says now, there was grit and sand in his genes.*

*Jackie was descended from a long line of religious
teachers in the eastern Pale of Poland. Rabbis. An
aristocracy of scholars. It was, however, a shabby,
threadbare nobility. The Mazas were poor, depending
for their survival on the charity of the community. To
the Maza door came generation after generation of per-
plexed Jews seeking rulings and clarifications on the
meaning and nuance of ritual and religion. Their homes
might be starved for bread, but there was always a book
in a Maza home. And deep into the night, even when
the stomach growled, the men were bent over candles,
reading, studying text and commentary. Arguing passionately over the interpretation of the various turns
and spins that life took.*

"Rabbi, can a woman lead the services?"

"According to the Bible, only those who have an
obligation to participate in the service can lead the
service. An obligation! As we know, women are periodically unclean. They have their monthly cycles and
cannot be obligated to participate in the services because of this uncleanliness, for how could an unclean
person touch the sacred Torah? It would be a sacri-
lege. So, if women have no obligation to participate

in the service, it follows that they cannot lead a service."

Such rulings and interpretations were essential to the community. Someone had to answer the incessant buzz of religious challenges and contention that arose among the Jews; there was, after all, no central authoriy, such as the Vatican, to declare church dogma. The Mazas became the clearing house for the approved behavior within their congregation. They might be poor, but they wielded the power of the book, and along with the power came, naturally, honor and esteem.

The Maza women, like all orthodox Jewish women, were relegated to a sideshow commentary on the commentators. From them came a pragmatic stream of common sense. "Study later, eat now."

Perhaps the counterpoint of humor was bred here, among the Maza women, muttered benignly like some psychic steam valve of perpetual exasperation.

With the practical release of sarcasm of the women and the spiritually devoted men, somehow the Mazas of Poland survived for hundreds of years as a credit and light to their people. Not that it did them any good in the end.

The Russians made no bones about it: They didn't like Jews, learning or no learning. To demonstrate this they made life miserable for them; they would stage periodic pogroms during which they would pillage and rape and slaughter the stiff-necked Jews who refused to convert to Christianity, who were always considered aliens. So, when the Russians swallowed a huge chunk of Poland in the late eighteenth century and there hap-

pened to be a large number of Jews already living there, it was politically awkward. To solve this "Jewish problem," as it was then referred to, the Russians simply demarcated twenty-five western provinces where the Jews were living and called it the Pale of Settlement. Jews could go on living there, but they couldn't move around the rest of Russia without special permits. Their work was restricted and their rights virtually didn't exist.

The town of Shmolensk in the province of Minsk fell within the Pale. Eli Maza, the son of a poor rabbi who lived there, like all his ancestors before him, as far back as anyone could remember, was a rabbi. But when the First World War broke out, it didn't stop the tsar's recruiters who swept through the province from gobbling up Eli Maza to serve as a soldier in the Russian army. Jews were permitted outside of the Pale of Settlement to stop the kaiser's army.

The Russian armies, however, were badly equipped and poorly led. They were quickly shattered by the enemy, which was how Eli Maza became a prisoner of the Germans. When he came home, after the war, the great turmoil of war had turned into a political revolution. There would be no peace in Minsk.

One of the wealthier households in the province belonged to the Gitlin family. They owned factories and land. The factories produced nails and metal hinges and the land produced forests and crops of vegetables and wheat. The hungry peasants were invited to pick vegetables from the Gitlin land during the periodic famines. It was a customary act of charity. But the Gitlin wealth vanished in the smoke and rage of the revolution. The communists confiscated the land and factories. The Gitlins were reduced to living off a small fraction of their former estate. Hands that never touched a hoe grew hard and thick with calluses. And Bella Gitlin, the youngest daughter, was no longer a sought-after catch with a large dowry. But Eli Maza counted himself lucky to wed a sweet-faced girl with a gentle and compliant disposition. It didn't matter that she had to learn how to cook and sew, that before there always had been servants for such things.

The Gitlins, for their part, were honored to welcome a member of the distinguished Maza family into the clan. Eli Maza was young, but already he seemed bent with the weight of all the books and learning and responsibility of his calling. He spoke, when he bothered to interrupt the long meals he packed away with such gusto, with unchallenged authority. And everyone listened with respect and reverence.

Eli Maza might have been content to stay in Minsk, answering obscure questions of Talmudic interpretation, and, like many of his relatives, he would no doubt have been one of the victims of the looming Holocaust, but he happened to have a father, Chaim, who saw that there was no future for a Jew in Europe.

Chaim spoke constantly of leaving, moving far away, and there was shock and consternation in the village. Leave? Move away? How could he just pack up and move away? Where would he go? If there was such things as roots, the Jews of Shmolensk had sunk them into Polish soil for the past five hundred years.

But Chaim was determined. Shmolensk was not the end of the world. There were other places for a Jew. Palestine, for example. Or America. Others had done it. He had distant cousins in a place called Portland, Maine. No, Rabbi Maza saw nothing but doom ahead.

And so he wrote to this cousin in Maine and he asked, "Is there room for one more Jew in America? Could a rabbi find a job in such a place?"

As the conditions grew worse, the trickle of Jews leaving Europe became a flood. Finally, a letter arrived in Shmolensk. The postmark said that it started out in Portland, Maine, U.S.A.

"Dear Cousin, you cannot believe the difference in a place like America. We have a small Jewish population in this town, but there are no pogroms. There is no fear of Cossacks in the night. The Jewish families here are now numerous enough to ask, Where is a synogogue? It would be a privilege to have such a distinguished rabbi, a Maza, lead our congregation. Come. A rabbi can live in America."

And so Chaim Maza obtained the necessary tickets, packed up his belongings and took his wife on the brave odyssey across Western Europe, across the vast ocean, depositing himself on that distant port of entry, Ellis Island. It was a sobering moment. The unconcealed contempt of the customs agents for the unwashed immigrants told Chaim Maza that America would not be a picnic.

But Chaim was a strong-willed, determined man. He had his last kopek sewn into the lining of his suit as he made his way north to Portland. America might not be paradise, but it was not Poland, either. And so, Chaim Maza became a spiritual leader of an orthodox synagogue in New England. Once he got established, once he got solid earth under his feet, he sent for his four children, wrenching them out of Europe, one by one.

It took a decade after the end of the war, on the eve of the Great Depression, when money was not easy to earn. *Chaim worked hard to earn enough to bring his children to America. He was the shepherd to his flock in Maine and he went around selling religious books — Old Testament, the Talmud, the books of commentaries — anything to earn enough money to bring his family to safety.*

Eli was the first to come — he and his wife, Bella, along with their two infant sons, Joseph and Gabriel. And they were amazed to find that Portland, Maine, looked like Poland. The landscape was stony and stark. The trees were isolated and strong, standing up to the rough winds that blew down from Canada. And the people were called "rock ribbed" because, in many respects, they resembled the landscape. There were enough Jewish families in the rural community to support a synagogue, to feed a rabbi and his family. But there were not enough to feed two rabbis and two families. Chaim wrote to the Rabbinical Council in New York City, asking them to find a job for his son Eli. It wasn't easy because oppressed Jews were pouring out of Europe in the last half of the 1920s and early '30s. Among them were a lot of scholars, many religious figures of esteem.

Finally, however, a letter arrived from the Rabbinical Council informing Rabbi Eli Maza that there was a job opening in another inclement corner of America called Sheboygan, which was located in the dairy state, Wisconsin. The heartland of America. Sheboygan was on the shores of Lake Michigan and was known for its cheese and its churches. Out of its docks went cheese and coal. In 1930, Rabbi Eli Maza brought his wife and three sons — Joseph, six, Gabriel, five, and the infant, Bernard — to the shores of Lake Michigan. It was a breathtaking three-day train ride — and it could be compared to the great journey across the great Russian steppes.

The weather in Sheboygan was harsh in winter and lush in summer. The natives were farmers or taciturn factory hands, with a midwestern reticence toward strangers. And the Jews were eternal strangers in their midst. They owned shops. They traded dry goods. There were no pogroms. No one threatened them with annihilation, but they lived apart.

There were less than fifty Jewish families, but they clustered together and became a community and provided a fine twelve-room house with a large porch for the new rabbi. It was there, in the house in Sheboygan, that the fourth and last Maza son, Jacob (who would become Jackie Mason), was born in that fourth year of the new decade, the 1930s.

His brothers remember him being rocked in his carriage on that long porch that ran around the house like the deck on a great ship. But if there was anything remarkable about his childhood, it was the reticence with which he faced his family. He had a tendency to blend into the background while Joseph, the eldest, shone in scholarship and family favor.

Rabbi Eli Maza could be as cold and unforgiving as the Wisconsin winter. He constantly warned his flock against the dangers of secular corruption. It was a snare that awaited them all. His scolding sermons rang down like Old Testament thunder. The Jews were never pious enough, never observant enough, never faithful enough for the rigid rules of Rabbi Maza.

"But Rabbi, I have to light the stove on the Sabbath, it's cold!"

The Talmud was very clear. There was no quibbling about the text. If a stove went out on the Sabbath, unless a human life was at stake it remained out.

The Jews of Sheboygan, like their Gentile neighbors, had a more flexible view of life. You could not last in such a climate unless you came to terms with nature. Unless you could bend. Life was a hard compromise and the rabbi who shook a castigating finger in their face was not popular.

The feeling was mutual. Sheboygan did not even have a yeshiva, and Rabbi Eli Maza believed passionately that his sons must have a religious education. Already, Joseph was eight; he was attending a secular public school. Where would he study the Torah? worried Rabbi Maza. Where would he learn the respect and awe for Jewish learning that could only be imbued, collectively, in a yeshiva?

The American schools, he thought, were soft and fatuous. The children spent half their time playing. They made pictures, instead of breaking their heads thinking of answers to the impossible paradoxes that made up the body and soul of Jewish learning.

"What about an afterlife, rabbi?"

"Some people believe, some don't. You can't prove it, one or the other."

"What does that mean?"

"It means, it's up to you. But you still have to live a good life as a Jew to be eligible. You can't get out of your obligations."

American schools didn't have the endless religious quest, the intellectual challenges that yeshiva offered.

Not in Sheboygan. Not in the 1930s when the nation was in the grip of the Great Depression and economic fear and religious orthodoxy held sway. All of these factors finally convinced Rabbi Maza that he faced a great hazard in Wisconsin. Not in the violent hatred of the anti-Semites. It was the risk of assimilation — conformity. The death of Judaism in America, he came to believe, would not arrive at the sharp end of a dagger, but at the bend of assimilation. There would come a time when Jews would become indistinguishable from Gentiles. This, to the Old World ascetic, was the true threat. Already he could see the sons of the fathers, the children, yearning for the secular payoff, the assembly-line goods that were so abundant in America. Already they had shed their dark robes and pious locks and dressed up in smart modern styles. They danced with girls, risking uncleanliness. They had to be dragged to temple to listen to the blistering reproaches of Eli Maza.

There was no way he could win this contest. At least not out here on the frozen ground of Wisconsin.

One day, in the late '30s, there was a great fuss at the Sheboygan train station. A mob was heading for the east-bound train. Thundering into the station was Rabbi Eli Maza, Joseph on one hand and Gabriel on the other, and there was his wife, Bella, pulling Bernard and holding their infant daughter, Gail. Where was Jacob? Eli was running for the train. As usual, they were late and it was a frantic chase to catch the Pullman. The sons were safely aboard. Joseph and Gabe and Bernard — but where was Jacob? Little three-year-old Yanki? Where was the baby boy? Then someone from the congregation, who had come along to bid the rabbi farewell, handed him up to his father like some afterthought, like some piece of luggage. He was safe, although, even here, not entirely a part of the family. Even as a child, he was self-reliant. Or, looked at from a different angle, someone slightly detached, without the need to clutch a blood relative as he ran for the train. Not altogether committed to this shouting, worried brood of wandering Jews.

It was a long ride back to New York City and the children still remember their father in his prayer shawl in the lower berth. Look, look, said the rabbi, pointing out the window. An adventure! Rabbi Eli Maza was, in many ways, childlike, himself, when it came to the American culture (which may be why he understood the danger). Once he took the boys to a movie. He couldn't get over it. "That train, how real it looked. Coming closer and closer and closer! Did you see? Did you see how real it was?" he marveled. "I thought it was going to hit us. I was frightened. How they can do such things!"

The truth was that Eli Maza was not entirely opposed to Western science and technology, but he had reservations. He was an orthodox Jew and thus he had a profound mystical side. Life might be explainable according to natural law, but the Jewish religion depended upon a deep belief in magic. A Jew had to believe in miracles and the inexplicable wonders that came straight out of the Old Testament. Bushes burned. Lands flooded. Pestilence and famine awaited. This was a hard lesson to teach in the secular wilderness. This is why he uprooted his family, gave up the nice house in Sheboygan, and dragged them back to the Lower East Side, an American shtetl. They would be among other Jews, they would see the delirious Hasids, ancient bearers of

36 · Jackie, Oy!

an ancient belief. They would hear the language spoken, see for themselves the street-corner peddlers with their prayer shawls and passionate eyes, feel for themselves the heat of five millennia.

The train pulled out of the Sheboygan station, and began rolling across the nation. The boys climbed the ladder to the upper berth of the Pullman and they couldn't sleep. They were too busy watching America roll by — an adventure! Their mother, Bella, would hand up fruit. Eat. Eat. Chasing them across the heartland with food.

We came back to the Lower East Side. I remember it. It was important to my father. It was important that his sons attend yeshiva, important that they should speak Yiddish and see Jews and not forget who they were. We might have been more comfortable in the material sense in Sheboygan, but this was not important to him. He was not interested in the secular comforts of the world. His life was in the Talmud. Learning.

They moved into an apartment on Rutgers Street on the Lower East Side — a province of immigrant European Jews within Manhattan. It was a first-floor railroad flat, four rooms, with children sleeping in every room. Bella filled it with dark, somber furniture, the heavy wood implying substance, but which cast a shadow of gloom in their apartment. Bella was a small, plump, self-effacing woman who retreated from all confrontation. Eli was a rabbi engaged in God's work and she had no right to disturb his concentration with such mundane matters as their poverty. He sat down

*and she provided food. If he said that it was raining,
she agreed. She didn't look out of the window to check,
she simply agreed. Why did she have to look out of the
window if Eli said it was raining? She did not complain
that she had given up a happy home in Sheboygan, she
did not express regret about missing the wraparound
porch. She put meals on the table and made certain
that the children were clean and she agreed with every
single word that Eli Maza uttered. She was too busy
preparing food or cleaning up to complain.*

*And the move to New York City was not without
blessings. Two blocks away there was a yeshiva. Around
the corner, the storekeepers spoke Yiddish. If you opened
up the window and closed your eyes, you could hear
Minsk; you could hear it right outside your window, in
the street.*

*The boys were enrolled at Yeshiva Tifereth Jerusa-
lem, "The Beauty of Jerusalem," on East Broadway,
two blocks from their home, where they became, in
their turn, acknowledged royalty — Jewish princes of
learning and scholarship. Each brought home awards
for scholarship, honors for the rabbi.*

*Except Jackie. He was always compared — unfavor-
ably — to his brothers. "Are you sure that you're a
Maza?" the mischievous rabbis at the yeshiva would
ask. "The rabbi's son?" No matter what he did, it was
never on the same scale as the achievement of his
brothers. But, then, at some point, he stopped trying.
He gave up. And the change in attitude did not go un-
noticed.*

My father! He was respected. He couldn't make a
living, but he was respected. The people would come

to him, "Rabbi, is this chicken kosher?" and they would hold up a chicken. He would examine it like a doctor and bless it and it would be kosher and they would leave him something. "Rabbi, the spoon from the milk dishes fell into the plate from the meat dishes, what should I do, Rabbi?" And he would look solemn and grim and explain how you could maybe boil this spoon for three days and it would be once again kosher. And they would leave him a jar of something. Or maybe a dollar. The truth is, he was living on charity. He would go to a wedding and after he married the bride and groom, he'd stuff his pockets with food and bring it home to us. It was no picnic. He wrote books, but they were scholarly books and they didn't earn money. He was learned, but he wasn't good at making a living.

My mother was a nice, gentle beleaguered woman who was the typical woman of the old Jewish tradition. Somehow, almost all of my friends had a mother very much the same type. She lived for nothing but her husband and her children. Her whole life was a study of self-denial. She felt she didn't deserve anything, didn't want anything, didn't ask for recognition or attention. Always pushing food on us. Did you eat yet? Always the same question. "Did you eat?" That's all I heard, day and night, who ate, who didn't eat, and she was always in the kitchen cleaning and washing and cooking and chasing us with food. At the yeshiva, she would come with a jar of chocolate milk and a bagel, to make sure I had something to eat just before school. And after school, she'd be waiting with another jar and something else to eat. I remember a few times being embarrassed, hearing the other kids say, "Oh, there's Jacob's mother," but I also remember being touched by it, how she knocked herself out.

Always trying to be the diplomat, because my father had a temper and he could get mad. He was always worried about me because I didn't study enough. "Learn!" he would demand in Yiddish. "Learn!" And I would lie and say that I had studied and my mother, she would back me up. Yes, she said, he studied, I saw.

I didn't have the stomach for it. It was such a long day. You went to school at the yeshiva from nine until seven at night. And then you had studying at night. And my father would storm and storm — "Learn!" He'd get red and angry and look like he was going to have a heart attack. I started to hate my brother Bernie, the genius. He skipped grades and already graduated from high school at the age of twelve. It looked like a futile effort to try to catch up with him. And the teachers would say, "How come your brother could do this and this and you can't? You putz!"

Already I begun to hang out with the boys on the corner, looking for attention in other ways. Already, by the time I was eleven, I was hiding the yarmulke in my pocket when I left the house, so I should appear American, because I would hear them when I was coming, say, "Here comes the rabbi's son." I hung around with the older boys and I went to the Educational Alliance where I heard the Socialists and the Communists and the Progressives and I began to move away from the family. I heard Bertrand Russell at Cooper Union, Norman Thomas, the Socialist —

great debates! Discussing important issues. The welfare of the masses. One world! Suddenly, I had opinions. The older guys were very impressed that this little pisher would have strong opinions about Roosevelt and politics.

Finally, it was bound to happen, my father started to resent me. "Learn!" he would say, and the more he said it, the less I studied. "Learn!" The more he resented, the more I disliked my father. I tried to placate him, I pretended that I'm turning back to religion, but he knew that it was a farce.

Sit down! Learn!

But I am hanging around street corners, shooting pool and learning about politics and boxing from Maxie Shapiro, a big hero in the neighborhood. A big hero. Maxie was a lightweight, a fighter, and he took me under his wing and he taught me how to box.

And always, like some tragic shadow in his path, was his father, pleading for Jackie to study. By now, his grandfather, a softening influence, had died and there was only his father and his unchecked anger, which exploded one night when Jackie was twelve. It began with the standard question: "Are you learning?"

Jackie gave his standard lie: "I am, I'm trying to."

Eli would persist. What, exactly, did you learn today?

"Look, I learned enough, I don't want to learn anymore."

Finally, he blew his top. He said, "Sit down! Learn!" I said, "I learned enough!" He says, "Do you want to learn, yes or no?" I said, "I don't!" He was flabbergasted. "You don't!? Why not?" I told him, "I'm not interested!" He couldn't understand. He says to me, "You're not interested in learning? This is the only thing we're on this earth for, this is the only reason for life. This is why God made us with a brain. You're saying that everything in life that means anything to me and your family for generations — the scholarship of our people — the learning, you're rejecting it?! You're telling me you're rejecting the whole history of our people, you're not gonna be a rabbi, a scholar?! You're gonna be a bum?! God means nothing to you?"

And then he started to pinch me. To bump me. I was a kid. Twelve. But I could feel his fury, his rage. "I'll teach you," he said, "that you'll never say that to me again!"

He was hitting me by now. I was screaming in pain and agony because he was hurting me. I remember we were in the bedroom and he was hitting me and screaming, "I'll teach you! I'll teach you! You'll never say that again!" Not curse words, but for him, verbal attacks. "You low-life! You bum! You common bum, filthy animal!" And he belted me and hacked me and banged me and I was choking with tears. I was gagging from crying so much and pleading for mercy and screaming, but it didn't stop my father. He kept doing it, intense, intense, intense. Hits in the mouth, banging over the head. He had hit me before, but nothing like this. This was a violent, crazy, insane type of beating and then, at the end of it, he told me, "Sit down and learn! You're gonna learn whether you like it or not. For the rest of your life.

No son of mine is going to be a traitor to God and holiness."

And I remember when he sat me down after that and told me to start learning, like it or not, I remember looking at him with vengeance and hate and saying to myself, "This is the end. This man will never get away with this. He'll never make me learn!"

CHAPTER THREE

The Smartest Kid in the Candy Store

No. He didn't give up on me after that, and I, strangely enough, didn't give up on him, because, even though I hated what he did to me and I had contempt for his behavior, and a side of me started to hate him in a way that I never did before, I also saw certain sick sides of him — the pathetic sides, the loneliness, the helplessness. I saw how he couldn't deal with life on his own terms in every other way, that he was basically a sad human being who, even though he was very prominent as a rabbi in the neighborhood, basically was an outcast as a human being. He couldn't relate to other people to be a successful rabbi. He could succeed as a scholar writing books, but he couldn't make a living. People were never quite religious enough around him and he couldn't deal with them on terms that they could enjoy or accept so, therefore, he couldn't even get a prominent job as a rabbi because he was too religious for this congregation, too uncompromising for that president of a temple — too severe in every respect.

I saw this tragic figure walking in the street, bent with loneliness, unable to earn enough to feed his family, always with secondhand food in his pocket and secondhand items on his back, taking what charity he could get. Someone gave him a dollar; someone gave him a candle.

And this tragic figure I saw walking in the street was my father.

Inevitably, there were alliances in this family war. The older brothers had already made their peace with their father. Jackie had spurned scholarship, piety — all the beliefs that they embraced. Even on small matters of no real consequence, Jackie was excluded, made to feel ostracized.

"We liked to play ball," recalled Gabe. "Punchball, stickball, basketball, baseball, whatever. Not Jackie. Joseph, Bernard, and I would go out to play ball and Jackie would go and hang out with his friends on the corner."

If he could not compete with them intellectually, Jackie was not going to give his brothers a chance to humiliate him physically.

There were, in addition to his mother, two younger sisters, Evelyn and Gail. The females of the family took Jackie under their protection, defending his independence, speaking up on his behalf, in spite of his often weird and inexplicable defiance. It was unheard of, the fact that he faked his studies and listened instead to the radio. But his sisters understood. They were, themselves, oppressed and excluded, as were all females in all orthodox homes. They, too, suffered exclusion in an environment where only male intellect was of any con-

sequence. Throughout Jackie's life, his sisters would always be his advocates.

Bella, his mother, kept her own counsel, but she seemed to regard her youngest son as if he were, as one family member described it, a "crippled child" who needed extra attention. Someone requiring a higher degree of understanding. When Eli thundered for obedience, and her son slipped away to be with his friends rather than study, Jackie seemed to strike a natural, protective chord with his brave and winsome rebelliousness.

"Ma, don't tell Daddy," he would say, leaving his books, running out to meet his friends.

"What if he asks?"

"Act confused."

"I don't have to act."

My mother was more concerned with my feelings than religion. She was more concerned with my survival. And it would hurt her to see me look unhappy. I had to run out of the house to get away from my father; meanwhile, she would speak up for me, so I should be able to live through this. She felt that I was being unduly persecuted by my father because she felt that, since I can't change that much, let's somehow try to make the best of it.

There was a candy store on the corner of Henry and Madison streets and, in those days, on the lip of the Second World War, the sharp kids would cluster outside and play penny poker and drink two-cent Cokes. Jackie began as "the rabbi's son," but gradually won a

*spot among them by his wild sense of humor and clever
wit and spunk. Like all kids, they would speculate what
they planned to do when they "grew up." In Jackie's
case, it seemed a foregone conclusion. Still, someone
asked: "So, Yanki, what about you? What are you gonna
be when you grow up?"*

*"I was thinking of becoming a Gentile. It looks like
a nice easy job and the pay isn't bad. Did you see the
girls?"*

*When one of these older kids — and they were al-
ways older kids that Jackie hung around — handed him
a nickel and said, "Here, kid, get me a Coke and keep
the change," Jackie handed it back.*

*"Get it yourself," shot back Jackie, establishing his
own territorial lines of dignity.*

We were all running away from religious tyranny
on the street corner of Henry Street and Madison.
There was a kid, Pinsky, he also had a yarmulke in
his pocket. He was going to be a court reporter.
Morris, a wild man, he became an accountant. Not
too successful, either. Morty became a teacher. Wild,
crazy, religious rebels. Staging a whole religious revolution by the candy store — and now look. Teachers and accountants and court reporters. I look at
them now and I wonder, "How could I have admired this man?!" I saw one not long ago. He came
to the show. A kid I used to want to hang around
with. A kid I used to think this is an intelligent kid.
But now, the level of his thinking, the degree of
awareness, look at how he's still on that same corner, never moved an inch!

And a leader! They were all leaders and I was a little kid, getting in everyone's way, a pest, and look what happens?

A couple of friendships lasted. A couple. My best friend from the corner was Bernie Weber. We called him Bushee because he had such lips like you wanted to kiss. Also orthodox. Also a yarmulke in the pocket. He became pretty successful. Had a television store in the Bronx. Then he went into real estate and got very rich, then he wound up managing actors. He's a big shot by now. On his second wife. Lost about a hundred pounds. Looks maybe thirty-eight instead of fifty-six. But I remember him as a kid. Bernie was always popular with the girls because he had colorful blond hair. And he always looked sharp. He'd dressed sharp and he acted cool. We'd go to dances at Young Israel and Bernie was always talking to some young, dark-eyed beauty.

I had to work harder to get attention. I had to be funny. Not that I minded. I liked being funny. "You probably think I'm short, but I'm actually very tall. And blond. I'm tall, blond, and handsome. I just don't like to show off. So, to you, I look like a short, dark Jew. But in reality, I'm a Scandinavian god. Tell me, what do you really look like?"

And the girls liked to listen to this strange, funny little kid. Out of my mouth came such insane flights of fancy. Of course, an orthodox Jew doesn't touch a girl. Even dancing was a very questionable thing. A couple of my brothers never even danced with a girl because they felt it's not kosher. A strictly tradi-tional, orthodox Jew does not touch a girl before he gets married, for any reason whatsoever. My parents didn't so much admonish me, but they let me know that they thought that this was not a good thing to have on your mind.

Although, I have to say that my mother was not exactly a prude. I used to do this thing in the act in which I talk about how I found out about how babies are made. I am very indignant:

"I couldn't believe it. My mother?! She's a quiet woman. Then I took a look at my father. Him, maybe. But he's got some nerve with my mother!"

The truth of the matter is that I was very young when I found out about sex. How did I find out? That's funny, too. You see, we always had a cat in the house. Maybe to chase mice — who knows. But we always had a cat. One day, someone brings in the cat and says to my mother that he thinks maybe the cat is going to have a kitten.

My mother looks at the cat and she agrees.

Cannot be, I say.

They all look at me. I'm very young. Maybe six.

Why not, mister big shot? asks one of the older members of the family.

Because, I explain, there hasn't been a male cat near her in months.

My mother beamed. Her face lit up. Look at this, she cried with pride. Already he knows about babies.

It was true. About sex, I always knew already.

Jackie was a teenager when World War II ended. He was still attending yeshiva when the soldiers came home and established themselves on another street corner — opposite the candy store. Life was still a struggle, but

there was a whiff of something like optimism, hope, in
the air, as if some great cleansing had taken place in
Europe. Jackie was thirteen, fourteen, and these com-
bat veterans were in their twenties, but their conversa-
tion was political, intellectual, and they didn't mind the
little mascot.

One guy had been in the 82nd Airborne, another
had been in the Third Army, another in Fifth Army.
One lost an arm. Now one was a teacher and one
was a salesman — all intellectual guys. Very bright,
and the things that they had been through! There
was one: Teddy the Irishman. Only one or two Gentiles in the crowd and Teddy the Irishman sort of
adopted me. He liked me a lot. He had no children
and I think I appealed to him. He looked at me like
a son. And the truth is, I looked at him like a father
figure.

Whereas some of these guys would think of me as
a kid — not a bad kid, a bright kid — but a kid and
therefore a pest and they didn't want to bother too
much with me, Teddy the Irishman would take me
to the Cooper Union lectures. He would say, "Come
on, rabbi, you come with us."

I'd hear the speakers and the arguments and it was
as beautiful and lovely to me as listening to a great
sermon by a learned rabbi. The interplay of logic and
ideas was what I had been thirsting for. To sit there
and listen to Norman Thomas appeal to justice, appeal to the highest, most noble instincts, to think that
such things were possible — that mankind could
evolve into rational, decent creatures, it made me want
to cry. I would sit there and there would be tears in

my eyes, knowing that life didn't have to be a mean, ugly struggle. That we could cooperate, share our bread, spread fairness everywhere. I owed this enlightenment and warmth to Teddy the Irishman. He was a truck driver. A longshoreman. A blue-collar intellectual. He was warm and concerned about me. He would buy me an egg cream and he would always include me in the conversations. He was a colorful character. A talker. Everybody seemed to like him a lot, he was a personality and a semi-intellect and he would debate and argue about everything. But he also had a colorful, humorous side to his personality.

It was an interesting group. A couple of Socialists, a couple of anarchists, a couple of Communists and the more I listened, the more I read, the more I began to expand and grow and begin to leave the narrow confines of the religion. I read John Dos Passos, the *U.S.A.* trilogy, and John Steinbeck, *Grapes of Wrath,* and I began to see that the world was a larger place than the Lower East Side. There was suffering and misery everywhere. But there were people with good minds who could make you see beauty and truth, too. You begin to read; you question everything. Everything . . . Even Roosevelt didn't come off so hot. After all, he turned back that ship, the *St. Louis,* and let all those people die. Roosevelt had his points, but he wasn't perfect. I could see, sitting with these men, talking things over, that the world was an interesting place. It was good to make fun of it. "Well, fellas, now that we won the war whaddaya wanna do tonight?" I got a lot of laughs. I got the approval I never got at home, I got it on street corners. If I wasn't a genius at the dinner table or answering Talmudic questions, I was the sharpest, smartest kid in the candy store.

At home, we established a kind of phony truce. I would pretend to study. I would pay lip service and go through the motions. And my father would not ask. He saw and he noticed, but he didn't ask. He didn't want to know. But I know that he harbored a secret wish that I would come to my senses.

I saw this very clearly at my bar mitzvah. We held it, like we held all parties, in the house. We had herring and the sponge cake and the sweet wine and it was a whole big festive thing with all the friends and relatives. Crazy Uncle Jake who taught us card tricks. Aunts. Everybody. I had a brand-new suit and I made a speech — a few scholarly-type remarks to show the degree of my learning and understanding — and I could see that this was a big, big moment in my father's life. "The Talmud teaches us that man has an obligation to lead a good life, not for any specific reward, not to win any specific goal, but for its own sake. We are obliged to lead a moral, good life because the universe inclines in that direction. Toward good. I am becoming a man and therefore I must incline in that direction. Morality." He came over to me after the speech and he hugged me. He never hugged me before in his life. Never. And then he kissed me. He never kissed me before. It's the only kiss I ever remember getting from my father. I was impressed. It was a big, big moment for him. A big proof that I'm his son and that he loves me.

But then it was over, the bar mitzvah was finished, and nothing really had changed.

Somewhere along the way, Jackie became conscious
of the larger society along Second Avenue. The famous
stars of the Yiddish theater who supped with the
threadbare, displaced royalty of European society. They
had their own round table at the baroque Café Royale,
with its thick wooden tables and filigreed decor. Di-
minutive Molly Picon, still wearing her stage makeup,
would drift down from the legitimate theaters along
14th Street and pluck a piece of Viennese strudel from
a rolling cart at Moscowitz and Lupowitz. There was
Morris Carnovsky, who, they said, could make even
dead stone weep when he played Shylock in The Mer-
chant of Venice, walking along the street, deep in argument with Luther Adler and Joseph Schildkraut.
Giants. The legendary Boris Tomashevsky struck the
same pavement as did Jackie Mason.

He would walk a few blocks from the dark, dank
cellars where the rabbis were engaged in their endless
quarrel with God and find himself suddenly in a world
ablaze with light. He would press his nose against the
window of the Café Royale and there, amid the red
velvet and plush carpets, was the great character actor
Menasha Skulnik, staring back. The waiters would be
half running back and forth with steaming plates of
soup or small mountains of fresh cream, and it seemed,
from that window perch, that all the world was lush
and rich.

The great critics and the famous commentators from
the Yiddish press would sit and argue all night in Yiddish and Polish and German and French, the languages
wafting like dizzying perfume over Second Avenue. There
was a kind of Viennese cultural richness to the atmosphere. There was intellect and art along Second Ave-

*nue in those robust days near the middle of the twen-
tieth century.*

*Farther east were the grim, gloomy yeshivas — fac-
tories for pointless learning, as far as Jackie could see
at the time. The rabbis, half crippled, bent over the
changeless text and their convoluted riddles. The stu-
dents growing blind with endless study.*

I remember Tommy Dorsey and his orchestra. As
a little kid, me and Bushee would run errands and
deliver groceries and save up sixty-five cents, because
for sixty-five cents, you could go to the Paramount
Theater and see a movie and then, out of the ground,
an orchestra would rise up! Out of nowhere. I can
still hear the announcer, I can still hear the announcer's voice: "And now, ladies and gentlemen . . ."
It was so colorful, so festive, it was the epitome of
show business. "From the Roxy Theater, Benny
Goodman and his orchestra."

I never dreamed. Benny Goodman. Glenn Miller. I
remember seeing Harry James. I would sit there in
the audience, I couldn't believe. The band rising out
of the ground, the music, so thrilling, so wonderful,
it made your hair stand on end.

*Once, Eddie Cantor came to pay a visit to Seward
Park High School. What an event! They had to have
police bring him in. Eddie Cantor. A Jew! Thousands
of people lined the streets to catch a glimpse. Stars
weren't so accessible in those days. You didn't have
television, with stars coming into your living room. But
Eddie Cantor was a great hero on the Lower East Side.
One of our own. You couldn't imagine. The tumult*

and the fuss — you couldn't even see him, but people thought they saw him, or they told people that they saw him, or they heard someone who saw him. It was an incredible thing.

Bands coming out of the ground. Eddie Cantor coming to the neighborhood!

I never even dreamed!

CHAPTER FOUR

A Stand-up Guy

My father was not without a sense of humor. In fact, he had a very fine sense of humor. Very Talmudic. With a definite tendency for the ridiculous. For example, he had a wonderful joke: "What's purple and hangs from a tree and smells like a rose? You give up? A herring. It's not purple? So it's not not purple! It doesn't hang from a tree? So it doesn't hang from a tree. It doesn't smell like a rose? So it doesn't smell like a rose!"

So, you see, Jackie wasn't the only one in the family who could tell a joke.

— Rabbi Gabriel Maza

By the early '50s, the nation was in the grip of a muffled conformity. Joe McCarthy's witch-hunting seemed to clap a stone hand over everyone's mouth, except for a few political humorists like Mort Sahl and Lenny Bruce. Humor was a way of confronting controversy while still avoiding it. It was the exact modus vivendi by which Jackie lived: approach/avoidance.

Joking denial. Just the thing he needed in the Maza house. Maybe, if he was careful, it was possible to back into his own home without causing a war. So long as he didn't raise the subject of a son's obligations, so long as he didn't argue theology, he was safe. As long as he pretended to be an obedient son who was making his way toward the rabbinate, in his own fitful way, he and his father could live under the same roof.

But it was only an eggshell truce. Eli's authority, while not directly challenged, went unheeded by Jackie, who studied less and less and spent more and more time with his friends. Jackie had embarked on a different road from his father and his brothers. His interests were secular. His life was more cosmopolitan. Theological riddles bored him. He didn't care what the Bible said about his duty. He cared what Truman was going to do with MacArthur.

The dinner table was a nightmare of breathless reproach. The family ate silently, without speaking, as if one word would shatter the whole edifice. No one wanted to cause the final rift, and so words that would have been unforgivable were simply not uttered. Subjects that were hopelessly closed were left unopened. Things had a way of resolving themselves without the dangerous confrontations that would have led to another outburst of violence or worse — an ejection or a dramatic walkout. As Jackie Mason moved out of his teens, a thick, sullen silence lay like a wall between the father and his youngest son.

In each other's presence, they were careful, polite, maybe too polite.

More and more, the beloved "Yanki" stayed away from his house, studied with friends, avoided the op-

pressive, undeclared accusations that made up the stone
of that weighty wall.

Well, I'll tell you, you could say that I was avoiding, but you could also say that I was more comfortable in a coffee shop. In the summer a house was too
hot. We didn't have air conditioning in those days.
A coffee shop was air cooled. In the winter, you had
to fight or negotiate with the landlord for heat. A
coffee shop always had heat. Two-thirds of the year
you were uncomfortable in your own apartment. A
coffee shop was a cheap way to find a place to sit
and have a coffee and talk unmolested for an hour
or two. For a nickel. But I could see where a person
could say that I was avoiding. It's not an unreasonable conclusion.

And when he was not in the coffee shops or the candy
store, or studying with a friend, he was attending City
College in Harlem. Studying the secular world, as much
as he studied the formal subjects taught in the class-
room. Eating forbidden foods. Dating girls. Tasting the
delights of the wider culture.
In order to become an ordained rabbi, a college de-
gree was essential. Since the yeshiva didn't offer one,
Jackie had to study at New York City's tuition-free City
College. He was still operating on the twin tracks of
pretending to work toward becoming a rabbi while se-
cretly plotting to become something else. He would take
long walks along Convent Avenue, studying the classic
architecture, listening to the voices of the residents
coming out of the windows. You could tell a lot by
what they were fighting about. Money, mostly. And

oppression. The frustration spilled out into the streets. Blacks suffered like Jews. He could it hear it seeping out like poison.

Jackie was an erratic student, seldom attending actual classes, but always passing the tests brilliantly. English, math, sociology — he had an innate understanding and grasp of the subject matter.

His brothers were deeply involved in the studies toward becoming rabbis, so much so that Jackie even took some of their tests for them at City College, where they, too, were enrolled. Jackie always did better on the tests he took in his brothers' names than he did in the tests he took in his own name. It was a matter of pride.

The ethical question didn't bother him. At the yeshiva, Joseph and Gabe and Bernard worried and argued and dealt with the high ethical question — Should a man take another man's test? The answer was Talmudic: If a man is engaged in a high calling, such as religious study, it is understandable, if not altogether forgivable, to have his brother take his test.

Meanwhile, in the evenings, to avoid coming home and facing his father's sullen disappointment, Jackie found other interests. He began to take voice lessons.

I was going to be a cantor. It wasn't quite show business because an orthodox boy couldn't really be in show business, working on Fridays and Saturdays — too many irreligious demands — but it wasn't quite the rabbinate. I started taking singing lessons as a teenager. My sister Gail paid for them. She was a secretary, or a semi-bookkeeper, and she would give me ten dollars to pay for the lessons. The teacher was an old-style European lady who lived in an Old World European apartment on 84th Street on the West Side. Very dry. A real prima donna. Very formal. She wore high collars and her head thrown back, looking down at you, tapping the nicely polished piano with her nails with an impatient look on her face that was like death. Her name was Zayde and she reeked of culture, and I felt like I had come down from another planet.

She would play on the piano and I would sing and she would tell me that my voice was improving. For the first three years, I thought my voice must be improving because this highly cultured lady said so and what did she have to gain from lying? She had to gain the ten dollars.

And I wanted to believe that someday I'm going to be a great and famous cantor, singing at the big temples for the high holy days. I thought that this lady is some kind of celebrity and I'm gonna take her word because it took from me the feeling of being the underdog of the family. It was a kind of escape from reality, when I would go for the voice lessons in that apartment on 84th Street. It made me think that I was working toward something glamorous, something important, and blinded me into thinking I could be something big.

Only, I still couldn't hit high C. In the fourth year, with all this improvement, with all this work and practice, I noticed a funny thing. I still couldn't hit that note. Sometimes you have to face facts. The plain fact was that I had a nice enough voice, but I did not have an important voice. Not something you could take to a big temple on the high holy days and make a living.

So, I left the lady with all the culture and the highly polished piano on 84th Street. I didn't walk in and say, "Look, lady, I been coming here for four years and I still don't sound so hot so maybe I better think of another way to make a living. Whaddaya think?" I dealt with it like I deal with most things that I find unpleasant: I just never showed up for the next lesson. I don't have the heart to look a person in the face and say, "I quit." I just escaped.

In 1953, after majoring in English and sociology and receiving a Bachelor of Arts degree from City College, having stepped outside the narrow concerns of the ghetto, having seen what there is to see, Jackie came back to the yeshiva — Beauty of Jerusalem — and took courses to become a rabbi. It was not a sudden conversion to faith, he had not had an inspired moment and dedicated himself to a religious vocation. It was another drift of fate that he believed would carry him to wherever it was that he was supposed to land. He decided not to decide. He would go along, pretending to become a rabbi, while checking out the rest of life's terrain. At night, he slept with his brother Bernie in a single bed and prayed that no one would discover his dual identity.

There was another consideration for Jackie's duplicity. There was his father. He could not bring himself to completely reject his father — not completely. Especially now that his father's health had begun to fail. Eli Maza had high blood pressure, he was overweight, he

*had problems with his kidneys. He was visibly ill, and
yet, when he spoke of his youngest son, there was a
glimmer of pride. A last ray of hope.*

*"The boy has a brilliant mind," Rabbi Maza would
tell the other men in the congregation. "Of all my sons,
maybe he could be the most brilliant." And then he
would say in that trailing, incomplete way: "If he ever
applied himself. Ahhhh! There's no telling what honors
he could bring to his people."*

*Rabbi Maza could take some comfort in the decision
of his youngest son to follow in the family footsteps
and become a rabbi; however, there were disturbing
signs he could not ignore about the extent of Jackie's
commitment. When he was still studying to become a
rabbi, Jackie took a summer job in the Catskill Mountains — the lush utopia of hotels and bungalows for
New York Jews.*

I started off at this hotel, the Pearl Lake Hotel,
which was in Parksville, in the Catskills. I was a busboy. The owner was this old guy we called Harry
and, like most hotel owners I have come to know
over the years, he was a difficult, cheap bastard.
Something about owning a hotel attracts a certain
type of individual, always looking to see how he was
being cheated, always watching to see if someone was
getting the better of him. Skimping, saving, watching
everything like a hawk, like somebody's out to murder him. Most of these owners are hard, crusty people. It's always a tough season, and it's always a very
tough row to hoe, having to make all your money in
two, three months, worrying about every penny, trying
to outmaneuver everyone.

If you got three days of bad weather, you would suffer. As a result, they were very tough on the help. Harry, like a lot of hotel owners, to save money, stuck all the help in one room and we slept together; all the help. They figured wherever you slept was good enough because they had a big gamble on their hands. They just wanted you out of sight. The guests were enough trouble. Very demanding people, the guests wanted to get everything, so they would be ordering doubles and triples of everything. I would drop all the doubles and triples, as well as the singles. It got very expensive for the owner and very dangerous for the guests. Mealtime became a real battle, with dishes and glasses flying and the owner screaming and the guests ducking. Let's say I was not cut out for carrying heavy trays.

So I slept in a lumpy bed in a crowded room; this was nothing new to me, since I slept in the same bed as my brothers when I was home. There were always a few cockroaches here and there in the apartment on the Lower East Side. As a matter of fact, I was better off in the mountains. The accommodations weren't wonderful, but again, who noticed? I was getting fresh air in the summer and compared to the heat and stink of the city, this was paradise. And the food was hard to describe, coming from a background where if you took a piece of bread you better eat it because it is a sin to waste a piece of bread, but when you are poor, to waste a piece of bread was just plain stupid.

In the mountains, you took a piece of bread and took a bite and threw it away. Then you took a piece of meat and took a bite and then you took a chicken

. . . there is no describing the sheer volume of the food. This is what they paid for, the guests. The illusion of voluptuous, bountiful tables of food without end. To boast, when you got home: "You had four main courses for lunch? We had eight and then we had the two-course snack before dinner."

I thought at first this is a place for millionaires, even though the people didn't look rich. Huge amounts of great foods with such a variety of tastes and flavors and cakes and cookies and this and that — I couldn't get over how great the food was compared to what I was accustomed to.

And I was a busboy, clearing plates, carrying big stacks of dishes for these butchers from Bensonhurst and the garment center salesmen from Long Island on a two-week vacation, eating themselves into a coma so they should get their money's worth. Carrying dishes for such a crowd was a murderous job. I hated the idea of physical work because, coming from such an orthodox family, the idea of physical labor was for somebody else. A scholar, a thinker, a philosopher, a teacher is something you would become because working with your hands is symbolic of not being able to work with your mind, so therefore it is symbolic of failure.

Needless to say, a person with my attitude about physical labor is bound to find some way of avoiding it. I was very creative. I dropped a lot of dishes. A lot of dishes. Harry, being the cheap bastard that he was, agreed with me that we should find something else for me to do. He didn't want to send me home. Because the truth is, he liked me. And the truth is, I liked the mountains. Even when I was a busboy, I kibitzed around with the guests and they would say nice things about me to Harry and he could see that I was an asset. Not if I'm carrying dishes, but otherwise.

Now, every hotel had a pool. And they were all very proud and very competitive about their Olympic-sized pool with diving boards and filters. The guests would sit around the pool, admiring it, comparing it to other pools at other hotels, but God forbid they should ever get wet. After all those breakfasts and lunches and tea snacks, they would sink like a rock. Harry made me a lifeguard. Perfect. Only one problem: "Listen, Harry, maybe it's not such a hot idea, making me a lifeguard."

"Why not?" he says. "We need a lifeguard and you need a job. It's a great idea."

"Well, Harry, the truth is I can't swim."

He doesn't skip a beat: "Don't tell the guests."

There was always a lot of entertainment in the Borscht Belt. The hotel owners were fiercely competitive and felt that they had to give the guests more and more of everything. A bigger pool. More food. One more event. If they had one singer at one hotel, they had five at the next. More is better. Most of the entertainment at the smaller hotels was home-grown: waiters who doubled as singers; busboys who became a band at night. One night a week they held bingo contests. Another night they had charades. A third night they showed a movie on an old projector in a house they grandly called "The Casino." And one night was amateur night. Always, there was an amateur night and the secret ambitions of

the butchers from Bensonhurst and the garment center
salesmen from Long Island were put on rough display
in the piny woods of the mountains. It was always a
sight, there in "The Casino," with the mosquitoes
buzzing at the screens and the secretaries dressed as
femmes fatales and the future accountants trying to look
like outlaws — and young Jackie Mason, looking like
Joe College, trying to be a comedian.

There was a lot of material, just from the environment. I thought of what's funny and I started to write
it down. Already, I'm a writer, now I have to be a
hit to the audience:
"How do you do. I'm glad to have been a lifeguard here because I don't know whose life I was
guarding, everybody else's life I don't know about, I
don't know if anybody drowned or not, because I
have no time to guard them. I was too busy guarding
my own life. I spent my whole time trying to make
sure that nobody pushes me into the pool because
then I would have to find a lifeguard to save me and
I'm the only lifeguard in the building. I would be so
busy yelling for help, I wouldn't be able to save myself. I hung up a sign: SWIM AT YOUR OWN RISK.
PLEASE DON'T JUMP IN THE POOL IF YOU
CAN'T SWIM BECAUSE YOU ARE ENDANGER-
ING YOUR LIFE; YOU ARE ALSO ENDANGER-
ING THE LIFE OF LIFEGUARD."
Well, it tore the house down. They acted like they
discovered uranium, I was so funny. And I felt very
much at home. I found it very easy to get up on the
stage and perform on that amateur night. And, as a
matter of fact, after that, I became the social direc-

tor. I was terrific. For one night. I only had material for one big night. But that wasn't the problem. The problem was that in these small hotels the social director had to direct all the social activities. As an activities director, I was the world's worst because I stunk in terms of athletic activities and I stunk in terms of programming. I hated to bother people to get involved in games because that was the job of an athletic director. An athletic director should tell people to play baseball. And, let me tell you, at the Pearl Lake Hotel, everybody is sixty-three years old and they're not interested in playing baseball.

The boss wants you to announce baseball. But announcing is not enough; they have to play. If they don't play, the boss looks at you: Ha! How come they're not playing? If I would come to the people and tell them to start playing, they would resent me for bothering them. He's bothering me to bother them and they're bothering me to tell me to stop bothering them! Because basically, they weren't there to play anything. They were there to sit. But the boss wanted to prove he has activities, to compete with the other hotels, and he's spent all this money on equipment that's just sitting there, so he tells me to start games!

Every time I tried to start games, the people got nauseous with the thought of getting off a chair. And, ironically, these same people who didn't want to get off a chair to start a game, if they saw that there were no games going, they would say, "This hotel stinks because there's no activities." This is exactly what happened. They would say, "Where's the activities?" So, you would say, "Good, let's start a volleyball game." "Not me! Play volleyball? I don't play volleyball." "But you said you wanted activities?" "I said I wanted, but not now. I'm tired!"

Jackie Mason could always make people laugh. He knew that. He could find the twist of humor and insanity in any situation. "Look how people take such pride in their car. Did they make it? They can't even drive it. But they strut and take credit, like they built this beautiful machine with their own hands!"

It was one thing to break up the guys on the corner with his improvised routines and another thing to stand on a stage and perform professionally, for hard cash, in front of the congenitally hostile Borscht Belt crowds (every member of an audience believed that he or she was put there by God to violently criticize every poor shmuck who took a chance and got on the stage). Jackie didn't suffer such failure, at least not right away. He felt the jolt and power of making an audience laugh in spite of itself. On a stage, he found that he could hit the equivalent of high C.

But more important, on a stage, he didn't feel stupid. Behind a pulpit, making religious pronouncements, delivering sermons drawn from the Talmud, he knew that would feel dumb. He knew that intuitively. He was not cut out to be a rabbi. Anyone could see that, except his father.

CHAPTER FIVE

How Jacob Maza Became Jackie Mason

"So this cop starts giving me a ticket for being double parked. I tried to explain, but he don't wanna listen. He says, 'Tell it to the judge; you're gonna hafta make a personal appearance.' Look at this, not only is he giving me a ticket, now he's my manager. So, I get before the judge and he says, 'Guilty or not guilty?' I figure, he don't know, why should I tell him?"

The second season, 1957, after he had been a busboy, he came back, ready to perform. And he was a sensation. For a while. But he didn't have enough material to come back, night after night, week after week, and lay the same audience in the same aisle. After he used all his jokes, twice, three times, he wasn't such a sensation at the Pearl Lake Hotel. They still liked him, but the audience was no longer able to protect him from Harry's obsession with "activities."

This is a complete and total lie. The truth is that I tore the house down with the jokes. The owner made a whole fanfare about having me there — a twenty-three-year-old sensation who tears the house down with a big mouth, a brand-new undiscovered comedy sensation — and the word of mouth is running all through the mountains. The trouble was the activities. On the stage I was great. The next day, I would start with the activities and I would stink again. And this man is paying me thirty-five dollars a week, plus food, plus the lumpy bed, and he figures he's not getting his money's worth. He wants the jokes and he wants activities. It got so bad that I would hide from Harry during the day. "Listen, Yanki," he would say, "I can't pay a full-time activities director and a full-time comedian. You get my point?" And, as I would start stinking the house out with the activities, a week later, he threw me out. This is why I went to another hotel. You believe me? Huh? Mister!

The guests at the Echo Hotel down the road ate it up much like the guests at the Pearl. But the material was fresh and Jackie was a sensation. Jackie tried to use fresh material, about driving, a subject about which he knew almost nothing, from personal experience:

"Be careful while driving. You have to be very careful. I don't know if you read about it, it was in the paper last week, that right now, in New York State alone, a man is being hit by a car every fifteen minutes. Now, I don't know who this man is, but if he doesn't watch out, he's gonna get killed. I am only trying to advise you to be more careful. My advice to you is, if you're driving anywhere, drive fast. You'll get there before the accident. And never drink while driving. Pull off to the side, finish the bottle, then drive. You could hit a bump and spill the whole thing. That's why I drive fast and I keep the radio loud. In case I crash, I don't hear the accident."

Jackie knew a thing or two about bad driving. He had, by this third season of his Catskill career (1958), with his savings, acquired a secondhand Hudson, a big clunky car, and when he sat behind the wheel, it took two cushions just to get his head over the dashboard. He had about the same amount of skill in driving as he had in swimming — which made him, from a strictly technical and actuarial point of view, a menace behind the wheel. Nevertheless, for some reason, he had a jaunty confidence about his driving. He thought, Well, look around, it can't be so hard, everyone seems to be doing it. The only thing that worried him was getting lost. He was always getting lost. Going around the block, he got lost.

So when it was time to report to this next job as an entertainer in the mountains in the summer of 1958, he called for help. He knew that the mountains were somewhere upstate, but that didn't mean a lot. That could be anywhere. He had no idea of where, exactly, these mountains actually lay. "Gabe, you busy?" he asked one bright Sunday morning in May.

"No, not really."

"You know, I've got this job in the mountains."

"I know. So?"

"So, the problem is, I have no idea how to get there."

"Why don't you let me lead you. I'll take Edythe."

"You'll take the yenta and I'll follow you."

Gabe had a Buick. He and his fiancée (who was vastly amused by the humor and antics of her soon-to-be brother-in-law) started toward the mountains.

One way or another, Jackie found himself behind the wheel of this large, powerful car and he was supposed to follow his brother Gabe, who was in a Buick. Gabe was clipping along the West Side Highway, still in Manhattan, looking back now and then, and, sure enough, Jackie got lost. He wasn't behind him. Where was he?

Edythe pointed; he was up ahead. This was not unusual, Jackie often lost patience, forgot why he was supposed to stay in position, and just charged ahead into the unknown. He was fearless. In any case, Jackie took the lead, not that he knew where he was going, and Gabe, muttering prayers, followed him, although the point was also lost.

Now, in those days, there was a low divider on the West Side Highway — maybe a foot off the ground — and somehow Jackie managed not to hit it, but to get two wheels on it. He was driving along, heading upstate, two wheels on the divider, two wheels on the highway. Slightly askew, but moving along nicely.

Edythe put her hands over her face. She couldn't watch. At 72nd Street, a highway patrol car pulled into the right lane and the policeman had an expression of horror on his face. Doom and disaster were balancing by a pair of flimsy tires (even though Jackie was merrily tooling along, singing like a lark, happily following his brother, who was behind him, on his way up to the mountains). The highway patrol officers knew that if they blew their siren they would startle the happy idiot half on the highway, causing an accident for sure. So they gently dropped back, the officer on the passenger side of the cruiser covering his eyes like Edythe — he, too, couldn't bear to watch. This was the way they drove along the West Side Highway and then up Route 17 and when they finally reached their destination, Jackie bounded out of his car like he had been ejected by a spring and declared: "Perfect!"

This is not so different from the way I ran my life. I got in the car and kept going, I got on the road to show business and kept going. But at the time, I'll tell you the truth, I didn't know where I was going. I knew I had to keep going, that I couldn't slow down or stop. That was my whole philosophy and motivation in life: keep moving, but where all this running and going was taking me, I had no idea.

Well, maybe this is not strictly true. I knew where it wasn't taking me. It wasn't taking me closer to my father. It wasn't taking me closer to becoming what he wanted me to become. On the other hand, it wasn't chopping it off altogether. In those days, I tried not to think about it. I didn't know, was I happy, was I not happy, I only knew that I was busy. I saw that my brothers had a low opinion of me. They were becoming more like my father. But for some strange reason, they wanted to be near me, too. They liked the show-business energy.

The brothers were like shadows of his father, trailing Jackie to the mountains, attending the shows, reminding him by their presence that he was in violation of

*the family tradition. The brothers had their own mo-
tives for clinging so closely to their secular brother.
Maybe there was some part of them that wanted the
show-business jazz, too. Maybe it was part envy. Maybe
they thought, at odd moments, remembering the joking
around the house, that they could be on the stage, too.*

I got fired from six hotels that summer. Bing! Bing!
Bing. I started to go up to managers because, by the
end of that season, I began to realize, it was very
clear to me, that I was very comfortable being funny
on stage and it doesn't take much effort for me to
develop good humor and to make people laugh. The
rest of it was nauseating and repulsive to me — the
athletics and the activities. So, I said to myself, when
the next season came along, because I was still
studying the rest of the year to become a rabbi, when
the next season came along, I'm off for the summer,
I figured this time, no more social director, I'll go try
to become a comedian. But every place I went they
all said the same thing: "You're too Jewish!"

This is an amazing thing since thirty years ago,
these hotels in the mountains are maybe 100 percent
Jewish. But they don't want a guy to come into their
hotel who's a Jewish comedian. They want to get
away from this heavy Jewishness. A slight Jewishness, good! But heavy Jewish was death. They wanted
to appear young and "with it" and American and
attract the sons and daughters of the salesmen and
butchers who were comfortable with the sound of
Yiddish. On the one hand, they wanted to be reminded they were Jews. On the other, they wanted
to forget.

To see it from Jackie's eyes, it was a revelation. His own father regarded him as a dolt and a Philistine, but here in the mountains, he saw these young, fiercely educated Jews as failures, doomed to become accountants or tax lawyers or maybe, if they had the hands, dentists. It was such a puny destiny, compared to the high ambition raging inside Jackie. He wanted the world to stop in its tracks, he wanted everyone to notice. He wanted more than respect — he wanted to be worshipped. He could still hear the taunting voice of his father: "Look at Gabe, look at the comments from the teachers, how it's an honor to have such a boy in their class. And what do they say about you? He doesn't do the work. He doesn't study. He doesn't pay attention."

Jackie would sit there at the dining-room table listening to the long lectures about his failures and derelictions. He would absorb the long list of consequences. He would not be able to graduate. He would not get a job. He would be a burden to his family, to his community. A shame to his people. Like a ritual, his father's verbal blows would fall, and Jackie would grow more and more stubborn and determined to disobey.

When he stood on the stage, when he made the audience helpless with laughter, he felt vindicated. The dentists and accountants had the credentials, but when he walked through the lobby, the girls became giddy and flirted with him, not their "professional" boyfriends.

It didn't matter that I got fired. It didn't matter that the hotel owners saw in me some mocky Jew and they wanted no part of me: I knew something. I had a secret. I am going where no one else is going. Straight to the top. Not that I had a choice. I have to show everyone. I'm going to be a star!

When the lobby hero came home to the Lower East Side, he was the semi-obedient son. He attended yeshiva. He studied the Torah. He would be a rabbi. Only it was fear and respect, not religion, that drove him on. He would be a comedian in the mountains, but at home, under his father's roof, he held his clever tongue.

Somewhere along the line, the impossibility of his position began to become clear. If he became a star in the secular world, his father would regard it as a complete lapse in duty. A shame and a sin. And if he failed at the sinful alternative, if he failed at defying his father and being a comedian, Jackie would be judged incompetent in his own eyes.

So Jackie did what he usually does when faced with unpleasant alternatives: he lied to everyone. He told his father that the comedy business was a joke, a summer job to earn money to pay his way through the yeshiva. Jackie called it "a hobby." And he told the hotel owners that he was stuck with this accent because he was half a rabbi and that was that, take it or leave it. And he told himself that he could make everyone happy.

I didn't lie. Maybe I didn't let everyone in on every detail of my life, but that's not the same thing as deceiving. Besides, I find that most people already know the truth. They know what they want to know and they don't want to know, they don't listen. Everybody in my family knew that I was a comedian. My brothers. My mother. Everyone. My mother's attitude was, "Did you eat good? It's up to you, be whatever you want, go wherever you please, it's not my business." If you looked like you ate, if you looked comfortable, if you didn't look miserable or furious or crying, that's all my mother knew. You ate? That's all.

When he came home, the family (those who knew) did not speak of it. Maybe this was an American fever that would pass. Maybe it was a phase. No one could admit that it was some lasting career. The thunder-cloud of Eli's disapproval was too much risk. He was the father, and in an orthodox home, that was close to being an absolute ruler. No one wanted to incur his wrath.

They thought it had nothing to do with anything that's rational or sensible. A late adolescence. I was looking for something to do because I wasn't comfortable being a rabbi. I wasn't that religious, which is a handicap in that profession. All my friends were on the street corner or by the poolroom, they were not religious. More and more, I was attracted by the irreligious crowd. They all had some religious connection, for example in the Young Israel, they all came from religious families, but this was a time, in the fifties, when Jews were compromising their religious convictions and they were running around with girls on the side, and they were even trying to have an affair, if possible, even though they weren't getting that far yet. In those days girls didn't even go that far with their husbands.

There is something that the audience noticed about Jackie Mason which was so far off from what they expected that it took a trained eye to spot it for what it was. It was this: he had very physical moves. He handled himself like a real boxer. And, in fact, there was some basis for it. When he was still a kid, there was a lightweight fighter around called Maxie Shapiro — the hero of the Jews on the Lower East Side. His manager, Willy Gruenes, would hang out on Jackie's stoop and one day he took Jackie to Gleason's Gym and suited him up in shorts and gave him some workouts and Willy thought Jackie could fight. He had natural ability. So Willy took "the rabbi" to fights and trained Jackie in the ring and it went pretty far. But when it came time to put on the gloves and actually go out in the ring and slug it out with someone else, when blood and bone were at stake, Jackie declined. It would have shocked his parents, the whole idea being alien to his upbringing. But the sinful nature also was an attraction. The contact. The fear. The risk. All attractive. All too dangerous. Jackie might have given up the bout, but he kept the moves and on stage there remains a compact glide to his movement that is reminiscent of a boxer in the ring.

I wasn't too sure that I could definitely make a living out on the stage. I wasn't that sure of my appeal. Or, to be honest, my talent. I was sure but I wasn't. I didn't know enough about the business or about the chances of a new comedian making a living. I didn't know how agents operated or anything about the practical side of the industry. I didn't know about other comedians, if they make a living or not, or it's only Bob Hope and nobody else makes a living. I was getting popular, doing comedy shtick, making myself a colorful character, but I never said that I was going to make a career out of it. I went to clubs. I watched other comedians. Jerry Brock, John Rogers, people you never heard of. I went to clubs and to nightclubs and I studied the way they worked. The truth is, I didn't work too hard at it because I still thought that I was maybe a rabbi. People would say, Well, you need a beginning and a middle and an end if you're gonna have an act, and I would say, Bullshit! I didn't believe that. I didn't believe in structure. You just get up on the stage and you sense what this audience wants and what this audience enjoys and you work to that audience. If it's a young audience, I could be talking about sex. ("I personally do not believe in sex, unless, of course, I am given an opportunity.") If it's a middle-aged audience, I could be talking about doctors and marriage. ("I was gonna get married once. Then I found out she wanted to live with me afterward; I don't mind getting married, I just don't want to live with someone.") If it's a hip audience, I might be talking about politics. ("I heard that they are going to raise taxes, which was all right with me as long as I was in school. Now that I'm making a living, pffft!")

The bungalow colony crowds were toughest. They were always last on the list of the professionals who made a living in the mountains. The entertainers started out a Saturday night at the expensive hotels, with their audiences of sleek, prosperous professionals and man-

ufacturers who had just put away steak dinners served by white-coated waiters. The mood was light and the laughs were good. One show at the hotel, then move on to another. Then another, and finally, by midnight, you were working the bungalow colony.

It was a tough test of a performer's metal, as he worked his way down the scale. The cheaper hotels waited longer. The audiences were already annoyed, knowing that they were not at the head of the line, feeling as if they were getting day-old bread. By the time Jackie got to the bungalow colonies — rough cabins in the woods where families cooked their own meals and the children were crying and exhausted by midnight — the mood was bleak and the laughs were like pulling teeth.

Still, Jackie was proving himself. The agents and the managers stood in the back of the nightclubs and casinos while he broke the ice in room after room. The accent didn't matter. The insult of being late didn't matter.

"Personally, I don't have to do this for a living. I have enough money to last the rest of my life. Unless I want to buy something."

Only the laughs mattered.

CHAPTER SIX

Getting the Borscht under His Belt

Emile Cohn was a mountain man. Every summer, Emile packed his bags and went up, high above sea level, and he didn't come down again until the leaves started to turn. Of course, Emile did not venture forth into the unbroken Rockies where he had to trap animals and cook his own food to survive. Emile lived at Grossinger's Hotel in the plush Catskills, where there were plenty of furs in the lobby, but they weren't attached to wild animals. Grossinger's, with its hundreds of acres and three golf courses, with four swimming pools and thirty tennis courts, with its long oak staircases where guests descended in formal splendor, was, during its time, the last word in mountain resorts. This did not exactly turn Emile into Jeremiah Johnson, since he was served his five or six meals a day on crisp linen and never had to change his own sheets, but Emile worked hard for his keep. He was the house comedian. On the shady side of the '50s, there was always a place for an Old World raconteur of Emile's easy style.

Emile told stories. He told about the rabbis of Chelm who pondered the mysteries and complexities of the universe and then applied their wisdom to man's daily enigmas. For example, how it could be that a piece of buttered bread fell one day and landed on the side that was unbuttered. Such a thing had never happened before. When a piece of bread fell, according to all known laws of physics and man's own experience and memory, it landed on the buttered side. This was the way God planned it. This was the natural law of the universe. This was the way things always worked. How could it be otherwise? The rabbis of Chelm suffered and huddled and thought. Finally, they had a solution to this mysterious puzzle. It was a great relief because the citizens of Chelm were getting a little nervous. With great fanfare and a lot of hoopla, the rabbis announced the solution: the piece of bread had been buttered on the wrong side!

Maybe at the Concord, with its fast, younger crowd looking for wise-guy action, Emile's kind of story would not go over big. But at Grossinger's (or at any of the hotels catering to a more mature, traditional crowd), it was a great comfort and produced a kind of happy sigh. The clever rabbis of Chelm always had a room at Grossinger's.

One Saturday near the start of the 1958 season, the owner of the nearby Flagler Hotel, where Emile also told his stories, asked if Emile would come over and have dinner with a new social director, a rabbi no less, who would be the master of ceremonies who would introduce him at the evening performance. This was how Emile met Jackie Mason.

As it happened, that weekend the Flagler was packed with a convention of kosher butchers. Maybe, Emile suggested to Rabbi Maza, as Jackie was still known, you could mention the fact that there were kosher butchers in the audience, but be careful; kosher butchers tend to be very touchy about their work. Don't talk about meat or, God forbid, the possibility of cheating a customer.

Emile was standing in the wings watching the young social director warm up his audience before he went on. Suddenly, his jaw dropped as he heard Jackie, always fearless on a stage, ad lib. "My mother had twelve kids. Boy, could that woman chop meat!"

An awful hush fell across the room as Jackie-the-trooper continued: "We have a kosher butcher in my neighborhood. You should see. One day, a fly landed on his scale when he was weighing a piece of brisket. I never saw a fly that weighed two pounds!"

It was as if an ax had fallen on his crowd. The butchers were red with anger. Jackie wisely cut short his warm-up: "Well, ladies and gentlemen and butchers, I guess that's really it. Now for some entertainment. . . ."

The butchers were not content with just getting Jackie off the stage. An angry murmur was creeping across the audience, even as Emile was telling one of his favorite stories, the one about the young couple who get married and visit the rabbi who has an infallible record for prophecy. The rabbi predicts that in nine months, the bride will bear a child. Well, in three months, the bride gives birth to a healthy baby. How could it happen, the rabbi is asked? You said nine months. Explain,

please. The rabbi thinks and thinks and thinks and fi-
nally asks the bride:
  "How long have you been married?"
  "Three months," she replies.
  "And how long has the groom been married?"
  "Three months."
  "Together, you have been married how long?"
  "Three months."
  "Three months and three months and three months.
That's a grand total of nine months!"
  The butchers didn't budge. Not even this sure-fire
material went over that night at the Flagler. The butch-
ers were still raw over the kid, the young one, rabbi or
no rabbi, who implied, or maybe suggested, or some-
how got across the idea that kosher butchers weren't
strictly kosher when it came to an honest weight. You
could almost smell the meat cooking out there in the
audience. Muttering. Threatening.
  The owner of the hotel grabbed Emile. "Get him out
of here!" he hissed into Emile's ear.
  "He's offstage," said Emile, indicating that he had
taken Jackie's place.
  It wasn't enough, said the owner. The butchers, with
their thick arms and heavy scowls, looked like they were
out for gristle. The owner shook his head. "I don't mean
off the stage. I mean get him out of the hotel. If you
know what's good for him, get him out of here fast!"
  Jackie was up in his own room. He knew that he
didn't go over so hot, but he hadn't quite grasped the
full negative weight of the reaction. He greeted Emile
with a shrug.
  "They weren't crazy about me."

"You have to leave," Emile explained, pulling him out of the room. There was a house full of very unhappy butchers who wanted Jackie turned into ground chuck.

"All right," said Jackie, sanguinely. "I'll just pack."

"I don't think you have time," said Emile shaking his head. "Forget packing. They are very upset; they want to turn you into chopped liver."

"They really didn't like me?"

"I'll send you your things."

He acted like the villagers were coming for Dr. Frankenstein with torches. I thought it was funny. Maybe not the joke, but the situation. Kosher butchers! They were kosher killers.

There were always more hotels down Route 17, the highway that led up to the Catskills. Jackie worked in steamy nightclubs and in mosquito-infested woods. But he kept working. Sometimes he made twenty-five dollars a show. Sometimes forty dollars. He refused to be discouraged.

"You know, you sound to me like you are a foreigner," said the owner of a bungalow colony near Pine Lake. The man had an accent thicker than Jackie's.

"Foreign? Me? I was born in Sheboygan," said Jackie.

"What part of Russia is that?"

Jackie came home with more than a thousand dollars that fall of 1958. He wanted to show his father, but it would only confirm Eli's opinion that Jackie had sold out to material corruption. Jackie spent the money, squandered it on friends and clothing. It was as if he

was ridding himself of something unclean. Some part
of him thought of the money as corrupt, too.

This was a time when all the neighborhoods in
Manhattan had what they called "cellar clubs." It
was a way of raising some money, having some pri-
vacy away from your parents, becoming independent. You couldn't rent your own apartment, not in
those days, so you had a cellar club. For a few dollars, you rented the cellar and you held dances and
you had a place to go. We had a place that was on
the second floor. Not exactly a cellar club, but it
served the same purpose. One room you had a dance
or maybe a few card games. And if you got lucky
and brought up a girl, there was another room with
a couch where you could be alone and do what we
called "make out." Nobody went too far in those
days. A little heavy petting, tops. But you wanted the
room for making out, just in case. It wouldn't look
good if you didn't even have the facilities.

But in our cellar club, making out wasn't so important. Making good was important. We had a lot
of people who wanted to be in show business. We
put on plays and shows and kibitzed. We talked like
big shots, like we were already halfway there, although we didn't know a thing. Bernie was like my
manager. He was my age but he knew how things
worked. He already had a business in the Bronx, a
radio store, and he had a sharp eye for show business. We worked on routines together. ("I went to a
psychiatrist. I wanted to find myself. But I wasn't
there.") Bushee was always pushing, pushing, push-

ing. He set me up in the shows. He kept telling people what a great comedian I am. Always looking for a way to get me noticed. Which is how I came to be Jackie Mason.

In the days before television talk shows, there were radio talk shows. And the Johnny Carson of radio talk shows was a tall stringbean named Barry Gray, who used to broadcast out of Chandler's Restaurant in midtown Manhattan. This was live radio, on-location stuff, and it gave the show a sense of immediacy. Like Edward R. Murrow broadcasting from the roof of a building in London during the Blitz. Barry Gray was somewhere between a journalist and a show-business gossip. His guests ranged from Bobby Kennedy to Jack Benny. And on slow nights, he kept things moving by drawing unknowns, aspiring knowns, from his audience.

Not that they were ordinary customers who stumbled into Chandler's for the meal. The people who came to Chandler's were hungry for exposure, not the food.

The boys from the club — we called ourselves The Stanwells; why, I have no idea, but that was our name — decided to get me on the Barry Gray show. I was still living at home, still pretending that I was going to become a rabbi and going to the yeshiva, but I was also working to become a big-time comedian. A big break was coming. Everybody said it. I was too funny, too hot to be kept on ice. Barry Gray would be my breakthrough. So, they bring me to Chandler's and they sent up a note (he used to take the notes from the audience to see if there's anything interesting, maybe he can get something going), and he says, "I see that we have a young comedian named Jacob Maza here tonight — could you come up?" So, I go up, and right away he starts in: Jacob Maza, Jacob Maza, how do you spell this? So, I spell it. He says, how do pronounce it? So, I pronounce it.

"And it's spelled M A Z A? Are you sure that's how it's spelled? You sure it's not pronounced Maser, because I've heard a lot of Masers but I've never heard Maza, with two long A's."

I could see that I'm getting nowhere fast here, because all he's talking about is Maza, Maza, Maza. "What kind of name is this Maza, is this a Jewish name? Are you sure?" And this is not the first time that this has happened to me. Whenever I meet people, I have to spend ten minutes explaining my name, spelling my name, then going over the whole thing again because by the time you get to the end, they forgot the whole thing. "What was the first name again?"

So, I said to Barry Gray, "Mason. The name is Mason."

"What happened to Maser? Or was it Maza?"

"I was just kidding. The name is Mason. *M A S O N.*"

Just popped into my head. I wanted to put an end to this name business because nothing I'm saying about a name is funny and the time on the air is going fast and so I said the first name that popped into my head. Mason. He nods, like he understands.

"So your name is Jacob Mason? That doesn't sound right."

"No. My name is Jackie Mason. Everything else was a joke."

Another name popped into my head. Jackie. In two seconds on the air, Jacob Maza was gone. Now I was Jackie Mason. Sounded good. He didn't look confused anymore and the people at my table, they were totally baffled. What happened to Jacob Maza? They looked at me like I'm a murderer — I just murdered their friend's name!

Jackie Mason hung around after the show and talked to Barry Gray. "Well, we got the name straightened out," said the radio star.

"But I never got to tell jokes."

"Never mind," said Barry Gray. "You're funny. That came across. Anybody can see that. Let me ask you, do you have management?"

Jackie had a bunch of friends with a lot of opinions, but he had no professional management. Barry Gray said that the largest management agency, as far as he was concerned, was the Charlie Rapp Agency. They booked the biggest hotels and the best clubs. The next day Jackie found the office a hive of cubicles, busy with agents and managers juggling two phones at the same time, keeping track of five different deals.

Jackie took one look at this place that seemed like a bookie joint and felt at home. Safe. Jackie didn't have to audition for Charlie Rapp. They knew about him. They had heard, because it was their business to hear. They had scouts in the Catskills. "You're gonna be a big star, someday," said one of the managers. Then he introduced Jackie to a young, Ivy League attorney who had just joined the agency. He would take personal charge of Jackie's career. His new manager's name was Bobby Chartoff.

In the summer of '59, when Jackie went back to the mountains, he didn't have to organize charades or game shows. He was strictly a comedian, not a social director.

My manager had me booked into Grossinger's. I was supposed to be an opening-act comedian. They gave me a room. Right near Emile Cohn, as a matter of fact. Emile told all the other entertainers what a sensation I was. But Old Man Grossinger, he never heard of me. The first night, I'm supposed to go on as an opening act for Emile, Old Man Grossinger asks his wife, "Who is this kid?" She doesn't know. She hears that I'm a comedian, but she couldn't swear because she has never heard of me, either.

"I'm not putting this kid on, an unknown, in Grossinger's," says Old Man Grossinger.

So, he bounces me from the program.

The next week, again, I'm supposed to go on as an opening act for another Catskills' star. But Old Man Grossinger, he still doesn't know me. He's not putting me on. Not in Grossinger's.

Meanwhile, I'm living there, I'm having my meals there. I'm working some of the other hotels — Pearl Lake, The Echo, The Grand. But I'm living for nothing. Old Man Grossinger sees me walking around and he wonders who I am and he asks everyone and no one has any idea.

Finally, he takes his manager aside and he says, "Listen, there's a kid living here, he eats, he sleeps, and he doesn't pay a dime. What's he doing here?"

The manager don't know.

Why is he living here for nothing?

The manager don't know.
Who invited him?
The manager don't know.
So, they came up with a solution. They threw me out.

In the early days, Jackie almost became a boulevard-
ier — already the sharp dresser.

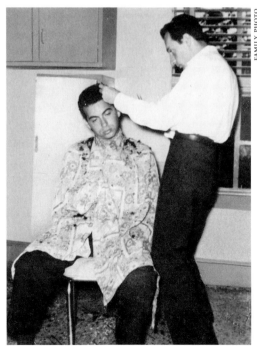

As a matter of fact, brother Gabe tried to cut Jackie's
hair. Gabe decided to remain a rabbi.

When he cut his first comedy album, a baby-faced Jackie gave it a modest title: "I'm the Greatest Comedian in the World Only Nobody Knows It Yet."

Jackie attempts to upstage the bride — his sister Gail — at her wedding. Gail's husband, meanwhile, introduces Jackie to a shtick that he would later use with catastrophic results on the Sullivan show.

The entire family takes a team photo at Gail's wedding. Back row (from left): Bernie, Molly, Gabe, Edythe, Shirley, Joe, Evelyn, Irving, Jackie. Front row: Saul, Gail, Mother.

In the early days, when Jackie began in show business, barbers had not yet perfected haircuts.

He was shocked to find that he was a hit when he started out in the mountains.

After the storm, Ed Sullivan welcomed Jackie back on his show.

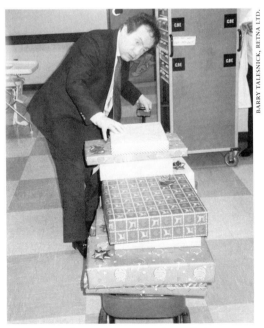

Jackie handed out Christmas gifts to kids in New York hospitals.

Eddie Fisher and Jackie shared a camaraderie: they both knew what it was like to rise and fall in show business.

Walter Cronkite never knew "That's the way it is" until he saw Jackie Mason in "The World According to Me!"

Jackie points out the relative position of Christopher Walken's stomach. In case he didn't eat yet.

Joan Rivers and Jackie couldn't talk; they could kibitz.

CHAPTER SEVEN

He Sounds Funny

I worked out like all comedians work out. I stood in front of a mirror. I stood in front of friends. I worked for donations in small clubs in Queens and in Brooklyn and sometimes the jokes worked and sometimes I bombed. I would see when I bombed that the reason was because I was trying to be like someone else. I'm not Bob Hope. I'm not Jack Benny. I could see this. I learned. When I talked about my own life, and I put on a funny twist, which was the way I happened to see the world anyway, it worked. This was funny. My humor turns out be very down to earth and I turned out to be the sort of character who laughed at the stupidity and insanity of life. This, they loved. "My mother had twelve kids. Then she heard that every thirteenth kid born in America was an Indian. And my mother's feeling was, Why should I have an Indian child? The Indian people don't have Jewish children."

There was a summer, one summer, the summer of 1959, when Jackie Mason conquered the Borscht Belt. He didn't just tear down a house; he moved mountains. He was playing all the hotels with a finely honed act, and the people didn't just talk about him, they gushed. The word of mouth ran like a fresh breeze through the lobbies and around the pools and at the busy mealtime tables. And something wonderful happened. Jackie was no longer just telling jokes and getting laughs — he could always do that. The character began to appear. A shape began to emerge. There was, that summer, a clear moment when he was no longer a stranger, when he stopped being Jacob Maza, half rabbi, half clown, and became Jackie Mason, that sallow, singsong, irreverent soul who easvesdropped on all of our conceits then performed comic arias on our vanity. The undeserved pride people took in a car. The hubris of having a fancy address. He seemed to be nudging us in the ribs and saying, "C'mon, take a look, isn't that ridiculous?"

There were other comics working the same intellectual soil — monologists like Mort Sahl and Lenny Bruce, who wagged an accusing finger in our smug national face. But Jackie had a forgiving aspect, a winning shrug, and he did not seem to sneer down from some superior perch at his guilty audience. Maybe it was the accent that stood out like a bald spot, a vulnerability that endeared him to the listeners.

He was up all night, writing out routines, trying out the material, unwilling to be caught short again. He would stay funny, every night of the week, if he had to. When it came to his work, he was not lazy.

I moved out of my parents' apartment and got an apartment of my own uptown, on 56th Street, although, when I say that I moved out, it's not completely true. I still kept clothes at my parents' house. I still slept there from time to time. I still maintained the illusion that I lived there, although I lived in two different places.

Still, getting my own apartment provided a very rich vein of comedy. That's when I started to develop the apartment routine:

"In the Lower East Side, if you wanted to throw out your garbage, you opened a window, you threw out your garbage. Everybody knew that garbage was coming. You heard a window go up, it was like an air-raid siren. People walked around looking out for flying garbage. But in these new, fancy buildings, you don't throw garbage out of the window. You have to take it to an incinerator. You'll find that all of these incinerators have one thing in common — you can't throw any garbage in them! Because nothing fits in the incinerator. You have to make sure your garbage is small. When I go to buy something, I don't care if it fits in the house — I make sure it fits in the incinerator. And you can't throw nothing in the incinerator even if it does fit because the incinerator only allows you to throw out certain types of garbage. There's a list of certain garbage you're allowed to throw out. The rest of the garbage you're stuck with. In my building, the apartments are filthy — the incinerator is clean."

As a social director, he made sixty-five dollars a week.
As a comedian, he got thirty-five or forty dollars a show.

But this time it was all show business. This time, when he walked into a hotel, there was a respect, a deference. People fought to be close to him.

I was getting a big kick out of coming into a hotel as the star comedian of the evening and going on the stage and watching all the people suddenly watching me, laugh at me, enjoy me. You could play small Kuchalains, bungalows with a stove to cook — a row of small, broken-down shacks that migrant farmers wouldn't live in, but they all had a casino for entertainment and on a Saturday night, no matter how shabby or small the casino, when you went in there, you still felt the electricity, the excitement of being a star. You got respect. On that low level, you feel like a big man if what you had before was nothing at all. Before I was a struggling social director, getting thrown out of hotels and now I was the star of the show. There's three hundred people, four hundred — whatever — and on a small level, it's a big thing. To a guy starting out, I was a big success.

There was a small caravan of entertainers who drove into the Catskills every Saturday night like an invading army, intending to slay the innocent civilians with delight, in that season, in the twilight of the 1950s. The acts, sharing rides, would pile into cars at the booking offices on 51st Street and Broadway in New York City where the last-minute objectives were handed out. Then they would advance in motorized convoys up Route 17 to upstate New York. In each car was a singer, a dancer, a magician, and a comic. You could switch a dancer for a magician, but there was always a comedian in the car. The audience demanded it. The cars had to have balance. They fanned out from Ellenville to Liberty to Kiamesha Lake, in time to make the first show, when the enemy guard was down, when the guests were logy with the heaviest meal of the week. The marauding entertainers would hit one spot, then trade places, move on to another hotel or casino, leaving a trail of exhausted audiences. The owners of the hotels and casinos stuffed their guests with entertainment in the same way that they stuffed them with food. It was very competitive.

The entertainers, unable to afford big-time public relations, promoted themselves, sang of their successes up and down the mountains. To hear them tell it, the Catskills trembled with belly laughs and applause. It was a mobile unit of singers and dancers and comedians, mostly comedians, who, for a time, provided vaudeville on wheels for the insatiable appetite for entertainment in the mountains.

Coming back, three o'clock in the morning, we'd all stop at the Red Apple Rest, which was the diner located at the exact halfway mark going and coming to the mountains. It was a big, twenty-four-hour diner with the kitchen always going and the lights bright and it woke you up when you were tired and coming home. It was Sunday morning by then and the acts were all still high on adrenaline, sitting around, kibitzing with each other — "I killed 'em! I killed 'em! I killed 'em!" No one committed less than murder. Could have been playing to an audience of deaf and dumb, wouldn't matter, they were killers. And I think that the only thing that impressed them more than who was killing who, was who bombed. "Did you hear who bombed?" Who bombed was a bigger hit than killing them. Doing good was nothing compared to being able to tell everyone who stunk. And they would always say the same thing: "Isn't it a shame who stunk!"

It's like an old man reading an obituary column and he keeps telling you every minute how sorry and how terrible he feels about who died, but he can't live without knowing who died and he can't live without telling you how sorry he is, and meanwhile he wants everybody to drop dead so he can spend his life feeling sorry. If they really felt so sorry they wouldn't spend so much time talking about it. Talking about it comes from the fact that they're gloating while they're telling you how sorry they are.

Part of the deal when you worked the mountains was that the hotel gave you a free meal. They would also put you up for the night, but most of the acts had other appointments and wanted to get away after the last show. If you stayed, you hit the homecoming traffic the next day. So the entertainers would head back in the middle of the night.

The Red Apple Rest was always jammed with bleary entertainers. Jackie would sit there in the Red Apple Rest in his usual detached manner, nursing his coffee, nibbling on his bagel, interjecting now and then, just to keep his membership in the group current, his own tepid boasts. ("I murdered 'em!") But he was young and most of the others were old and tired and when he looked ahead, he saw only a steady improvement. He could not imagine that he would end up going from table to table, whining about his rotten luck like the worst of these disappointed old performers. But he listened to the complaints and enjoyed the society of the other comics. There was the gentle Larry Best and Lou Menschel, both dead now. Menschel usually held court. He was the true Borscht Belt comedy veteran. He was a man who, for twenty years, right up until the moment he died, was preparing his material for Carson. What should he include? What should he toss out? Not that he ever made it to the Carson show. Not that there was ever a prayer. But it paid to be ready. Just in case. You never know.

There were a lot of old timers like Menschel, waiting to be discovered.

He was a staple in the mountains for many, many years and he was a very funny guy. He had ambition — we all had ambition — but he didn't know how to express it and he never really got anywhere in his career and he became one of the standard comedians in the mountains. He was ten times funnier than the stars. And he was very well liked, as a comedian.

As a person he had the same jealousies about who's making it and he was full of the same rationalizations about why he's not making it; that he doesn't want to make it, that he doesn't need it: "These successful guys are struggling but they're getting nothing out of it but I have such a great life. I have my own home, I have my own car, you know how much money I got?" Then he would give you facts and figures to prove to himself and to you that he's doing really great, even though you can't tell, and that he doesn't need it because it's a miserable life to be such a success. Failure is really better and flopping is really a hit and this low-class level of show business is more peaceful, more contentment, he doesn't have to be involved in a rat race.

But with all these rationalizations, it was still bothering him that he wasn't such a hit. So he used to walk around, always talking about who bombed or where they bombed or why they bombed or how they bombed. 'Cause when a big shot bombed, it made him feel comfortable that he's not such a big hit.

I'll never forget, he always said, "I'm so happy for people when they do good. I love to see people who do good. When people do good, it doesn't take nothing away from me. When somebody does good in show business, it's better for everybody. Doesn't hurt me. It does me good. My heart fills with warmth and love and happiness. I'm never so happy as when I see someone else doing good. That's why it hurts me that I just found out that Dick Shawn just bombed in London! You have no idea how terrible I feel. He's such a sweet, wonderful guy and to hear that he bombed in London makes me feel terrible."

Menschel takes out an article from a London newspaper that he went to buy special because he felt so terrible that Dick Shawn bombed in London, he wanted to read it himself. And not only that, he felt so terrible that he couldn't stop carrying it around in his pocket, this article from a London newspaper, and relive how terrible he feels every time he met somebody. And as soon as he saw me sitting there he took out this article and showed it to me and he says, "Isn't it terrible that Dick Shawn bombed in London? It hurts me to see it, look! Look!"

When Jackie came home, after the season . . . but where was his home? Jackie had his own apartment and he had a bed in his parents' home on Henry Street. He had long since completed the five-year course of study to become a rabbi, he had been tested orally and in written examinations on Jewish philosophy and history and theology; he had studied thousands of commentaries on the Talmud and been ordained a rabbi in 1958. Officially, he was a rabbi, a teacher. He could adjudicate religious law, civil disputes between Jews. He could perform weddings, supervise bar mitzvahs. He could console the sick and comfort the bereaved. He was entitled to represent the Jewish community to the outside world. But it always took the same comic form when he tried. In the most solemn moments Jackie had a wisecrack. Looking at a dead body once when he was called upon to handle a funeral, he said to the shocked undertaker: "He don't look so bad, you sure this guy's dead?"

He was a rabbi during the high holy days at the Concord Hotel, but his sermons were always brightened by the impious twinkle that came from the mind of a professional comedian.

"You know, nowadays, people live for material things. They have to have a new car every year, a good vacation, a new home. They spend their whole life worrying about do they have more than the people next door. I would like to leave this congregation with a thought that was told to me by my grandfather — a spiritual man. He told me never guard your money. Guard your health. A wise man. So, one day, while I was busy guarding my health, somebody stole all my money. Turned out to be my grandfather. I found out, that's how he made a living. So, I say to this congregation, Don't worry about guarding your health, guard your grandfather."

The people at the Concord Hotel laughed. They looked around afterward and checked and everyone else was laughing. And looking around. What were they, an audience or a congregation? What kind of a rabbi was this? Not even Jackie knew. Everything about him waffled in those years. His father would come to him — frail now, sick, bent with disease — and pose the unspoken question: So? Are you a rabbi or are you a comedian? And Jackie would avert his eyes.

The people on the Lower East Side would come back from the mountains and they would say, "Rabbi Maza, your son is so popular. Rabbi Maza, your son is in all the hotels. You should hear! You should see!" But Rabbi Maza couldn't hear and he refused to see. Like the rabbis of Chelm, Rabbi Maza tried to find some answer to this conundrum: Is Yanki a rabbi or a comedian?

Both. For a while, he tried to perform both jobs. In the summers, he worked the mountains. In the winters, he worked the pulpit. He got his first job as a rabbi through his brother.

When Gabe was a student rabbi, he was the spiritual leader of a small Jewish congregation in Weldon, North Carolina. They couldn't afford a full-time rabbi, so when

*Gabe moved on, taking on a full-time job in Pennsyl-
vania, he handed over his part-time job to Jackie.*

*Eli saw that Jackie's indecision was rooted in some-
thing far deeper than a poor-paying part-time job. He
suspected a crisis of faith. When he confronted his son,
when he asked about all this business in the mountains,
Jackie insisted that it was a hobby. He said that he
didn't earn enough as a rabbi and the comedy paid better than the usual part-time jobs he could get to sup-
plement his income.*

I told him that I didn't want to sell shoes — which
I had to do when I was serving in a congregation in
North Carolina. I make more money at telling jokes
than at selling shoes. As far as making a living as a
rabbi, I was only a part-time rabbi and I could not
make a living. "Is it so terrible? Is it more pious to
sell a shoe than a joke?" I am really a rabbi.

Of course, this is a complete and total lie and I am
certain that he knew it. I am also certain that he could
not face the fact that his son had strayed so far and
become a show-business bum.

*In the winter of 1959, Rabbi Eli Maza died. He wasn't
old when he died — just short of sixty. But he had high
blood pressure and he was overweight and he refused
to slow down or stop overeating.*

*When his father died, Jackie rushed from his apart-
ment on 56th Street. He was overcome with guilt. He
felt as if he personally caused the stroke by his continued defiance of his father's will. While all the other
members of the family sat shiva — the traditional gath-*

ering of mourners on wooden crates — Jackie withdrew into his room. He stayed there for more than a
week, refusing to come out, refusing to display his grief.
Finally, at the end of the period of mourning he
emerged — pale, trembling, having buried his father in
his own way. But it didn't work. Rabbi Eli Maza —
wagging that accusatory finger — would remain with
his son forever.

CHAPTER EIGHT

TV or Not TV?

First, I was a rabbi in a place called Weldon, North Carolina. Five Jews in the whole town and they don't even want you to know that they're Jews. They're so outnumbered, they can't even afford a full-time rabbi. Only a part-time student rabbi. Gabe was a student rabbi there first, then when he left, he turned over this congregation to me. This is 1959, 1960.

I don't know if I helped anybody spiritually, but I got a few laughs. Then I was a rabbi in my brother Gabe's second temple in Latrobe, Pennsylvania. Also not a lot of Jews. Not even a year that lasted. I tried, but I couldn't be serious. More and more jokes, less and less sermon. I had Gentiles coming to hear the sermons, that's how funny I was. I know that I use this in the act, but it happens to be true. Gentiles actually came to hear the sermons. Maybe not a lot, but even a couple is a lot.

But there was one sermon I gave which convinced me, when I knew that I was totally useless as a rabbi. Already I had a little reputation as a rabbi with a roving eye and I started to deliver this very solemn sermon about the need for a spiritual dimension to a person's life:

"The problem with people is that they give in to the ways of the flesh," I said. "They concentrate on the physical side and neglect the spiritual needs of a human being."

Just my luck, at that moment, in walks a beautiful blonde. She's late and she makes an entrance and I look up from the text and I completely lost my place. In all my years as a comedian, I never got a bigger laugh. That's when I knew, I better get out of this rabbi business.

The out-of-town flops convinced him: Jackie quit the rabbinate after three frustrating years. Besides, now that his father was dead, there was no need to keep up the pretense of piety. Finished. It was better to have a clean break.

Now he had the Charlie Rapp Agency representing him, now he could count himself a true "professional." Charlie Rapp, who booked the acts for two hundred hotels in the Catskills alone, was known as the "King of the Mountains." And he liked Jackie. But then, Charlie always had a warm spot for the comics. In fact, the short, dapper agent never went anywhere without one quick wit at his left side, whispering lines into his good ear. Even when he went across the street to Hanson's restaurant, he brought a comedian. They weren't always the best stage comedians — it was a cruel truth that guys could be funny at the table and die up on the stage. But Charlie kept them around, the same way he carried an unlit cigarette, as a prop, a piece of business.

One year it was Gene Bayliss. The next the hot comic was Corbett Monica. And then it was Jackie Mason. In 1960, Jackie Mason was rookie of the year.

"I like this boy," said Charlie, anointing Jackie, who was not blind, who counted himself blessed because he could look out in the waiting room and see the sad cast of show-business characters — over-the-hill singers, nervous magicians, tired dancers — all with that death mask, like they'd been sitting there for four days waiting to see Charlie Rapp. Jackie didn't have to go through that kind of day-surgery. He just launched himself as a full-time, no-holds-barred comedian and Charlie was ready to help. He told his brightest, best, new assistant to inform Jackie on the facts of show-business life. Bobby Chartoff was a young, soft-spoken lawyer with Ivy League polish. But his most impressive credential was that he was smart. He had a canny grasp of how things worked. One day, in the spring of 1960, he took Jackie across the street to Hanson's, and, over lunch, explained the world that Jackie was about to enter.

They sat in the noisy, midtown cafeteria over tuna fish sandwiches and coffee and Bobby said big-time bookings were a long way off. There would still be the Catskill hotels in the summer — Grossinger's, the Concord — where he would open the show for the big-name acts. But, be patient, counseled Chartoff. New areas were opening up. The Poconos and the Berkshires, the Italian Alps, were beginning to book shows. The money wasn't as good as it was in the Catskills, but it took up some slack in the off season and would give him work before Gentile crowds. For a while, Jackie would have to ride the small-time circuit, the minor leagues of show business. Take the time, said Chartoff. Polish the act.

Spread your name, see how the country takes to you.
It'll be a trial marriage.

Jackie saw the wisdom of the advice. He was, for the
moment, a small-time act. Small-time was Broadway
Danny Rose scuffling, playing nightclubs where they
watered the drinks and mob killers got the best tables.
Small-time was working in rooms with crashing silver-
ware and loud conversations and taking whatever pay
was offered. Small-time was doing ninety minutes at a
bar mitzvah where you have to introduce all the rela-
tives, and the parents, the people who paid you, looked
like they weighed the jokes like customers watching a
scale. They gave you back tight, grudging smiles in-
stead of laughs as if every sign of appreciation cost
something.

Small-time was driving down to Miami like a bomber
pilot with maybe enough gas to make it, then working
sleazy clubs for twenty-five dollars a show, then com-
ing home on empty. Hard, dull migrant labor with no
visible prospects and only the sagging examples of de-
feat all around you.

The Golden Nights was located on the fringe of Miami
Beach, down near one of the crossover bridges into
Miami itself. A low-slung blockhouse with no windows
and a big, red crude sign announcing that there was
"Entertainment Tonight!" The drinks were a buck and
the women slouching at the bar not much more.

"Hello, hello! My name is Jackie Mason and, if
you can believe it, I'm the comedian. Don't worry if
you never heard of me, I never heard of you, either."

You didn't have much time in a place like the Golden
Nights. Maybe a minute. If you didn't catch them with

that first burst of one-liners, you lost them. They stared at you, through the haze and smoke and fog of liquor and drugs, like fish.

"I'll tell you the truth, I'm not used to working in such a fancy club. Usually, I have to entertain in miserable places you wouldn't believe. The last place was so bad that business picked up when they had a fire. They sold water."

All the while, Jackie was doing graduate work on comedy. Learning the pitch and tone of a joke — holding back a punch line until the tension broke like a rubber band. Feeling the power of that kind of control. He came to understand something all good comedians come to know — the texture of an audience — the late crowds full of hecklers and drunks, the early crowds, hungry and impatient. He became a sailor who senses the tides, a hunter who hears the laughs before they even begin. And even during the worst of it, even when he had to go on stage wearing a stained jacket and a threadbare shirt, even when there was no one out there but a few dazed bodies, even then he loved it like a child. Even when it was bleak and sordid and dangerous, it was still show business.

"Fires must be good for business. That's why they have fire sales. I heard the owner tell a guy that a fire wouldn't hurt this place too much. He was telling a guy holding a can of gasoline."

And always, this forest creature had an ear to the ground listening for the sound of an opportunity. Listening and sniffing the wind and moving in the direc-

tion he hoped would lead him to the safety of stardom.
The sanctuary of being a hit. The expression they use,
not for nothing, is having "arrived."

I was already a hit in the mountains. A hit is making a hundred, hundred and twenty-five a show. Four
shows a night, it adds up. I was making sometimes
five thousand dollars in a season and for me, coming
out of poverty and misery, it was like wealth. I knew
that I could make a living in the summer, but I wanted
to know if I could make a living all year round. I
said, "It's time for me to try to play in a Gentile-type
club." To see if I could make it in a wider world.
Everybody said, "Impossible!" With my accent, to
play in front of Gentiles? Impossible. They said this
when I said that I wanted to play in the mountains.
In front of Jewish audiences. They said I was too
Jewish for that. You can imagine how Jewish they
felt I was in terms of Gentiles. They thought I would
be ridiculous altogether.

Bobby Chartoff and I hit it off together. He was
maybe a couple of years younger than I was and he
didn't seem to have the same type of hangups like
the others. He thought maybe I could play different
crowds. He thought I was funny. He wasn't officially
my manager, but he worked in the agency and we
started to talk together about the future. On his own,
he was talking to the nightclub owners or the agents
representing the nightclub owners, saying maybe
they're missing a bet here, and they said, "Too
Jewish!"

What is it, I kept asking? What could it be?

Bobby says, I'll be honest, they say it's the accent.

Impossible, I say, the accent is perfect.

He looks at me like I'm nuts.

By now, Bobby is hearing this accent business so much, he begins to believe it. He says, there's so much resistance, maybe it pays to talk better, maybe we should do something about the accent. Maybe you should just look into it. It could be holding you back.

We had some debates. First, he's not so sure and he's just exploring and he was very disturbed because he felt that I was hilarious and he couldn't understand why I wasn't getting my feet off the ground. He couldn't get a booking and he was frustrated. I kept insisting that we shouldn't get a verdict by some extraneous, preposterous issue, that it doesn't hold any water to me and is just a cliché from these idiots who don't know the difference because whenever I play to Gentiles, they're laughing their heads off. I played in the Italian mountains, in the Poconos, in the Berkshires, in Pennsylvania, and I used the same material and the same jokes and I got the same laughs.

But, listen, it didn't matter, I wasn't going to change my accent, I don't care what kind of an argument I got. I was happy. I was still playing the Concord. I was still making a nice living. I wasn't going to go hungry. If it takes a little longer, so it takes a little longer.

There was a hot club in California run by three brothers, a comedy trio, called the Slate Brothers. They were a vaudeville act — singing, dancing, jokes — and when they became middle-aged and could no longer jump around the stage, they opened their own night-club on La Cienega Boulevard in Beverley Hills. It be-

came an instant show-business imperative. Don Rickles
became a quick hit there. Jackie sensed an opening.

A certain comedian was playing there and me and
Charlie Rapp and Bobby Chartoff began to beg this
particular comedian to put in a good word for me.
We knew that the Slate Brothers had heard of me,
they heard that I was funny, but they heard also that
I'm too Jewish. Finally, suggestions, pleading, and we
get an offer. They'll give me three hundred dollars a
week but they don't want to give me more than a
one-week contract in case I stink. They want to be
able to get rid of me right away because they felt I'd
probably be too Jewish for their crowd.

Okay, that's what it was, so I'll take a chance. I
flew out to California on my own money and I moved
into a motel a few blocks away from the club. I was
a little nervous, but not much. I came into the club
and I looked at the room and I had a tape recorder
and I tested my jokes and I thought, I'll do fine. I
had my material. I didn't change the jokes. Shuffle
the order, maybe, but not much change. The jokes
were good. An apartment is funny. A doctor is funny.
I didn't think that people in California were so different from people in New York. A laugh is a laugh,
funny is funny. I met the Slate Brothers and they were
cordial — not too friendly, in case they have to fire
me, I don't think they had much confidence that I'll
be a hit.

It was a Wednesday night and there were maybe a
hundred people in the house and I started out with a
routine about sex:

"I didn't know how I came into this world until I was twenty. That's when I found out. I couldn't believe it. I kept saying to myself, 'My mother!?' My mother's a quiet woman who all her life she kept cooking and cleaning, cleaning and cooking. I said to myself, 'When did she have time?' Then I took a look at my father and I said to myself, 'Him, maybe.' "

It got screams. This was one of my big, big routines and the timing had improved, gotten better and better as I worked on it and I know it's sure-fire. The rest of the act went over, too:

"Did you know that my grandfather was the original signer of the Declaration of Independence? And don't think it was easy for him to sign it because he was living in Poland at the time. I'll tell you some more about my family. Did you ever hear of General Custer with his last stand? Do you know that my uncle had a stand right next to General Custer? I'll tell you another thing. Did you ever hear of the Boston Tea Party? Who do you think was the caterer?"

The material, even the one-liners, played well and the accent was not a problem. In fact, the accent enhanced the flavor of the jokes. It was something that Jackie always knew. The thing that he was perfecting was the timing. That vital pause between lines when the audience has already laughed at that first set-up, when they are already convinced that they'd had the payoff, and then they are caught by the second stage, that zinger: ("My mother, never! She's a nice, quiet woman, always cooking and cleaning, cleaning and cooking." Pause. "Then I took a look at my father and

I said to myself, 'Him, maybe!' ") Wait too long and it's gone. Come in too quick and you step on your own laugh. Timing requires a lot of nerve and it has to be perfect. Jackie already had natural gifts in that department, but he was learning the nuances of just how far timing could take him.

Bobby Chartoff had come out for the opening. After the first performance in this club, with its tables as small as pinheads and it's button-down clientele, while Jackie and Bobby were still in the dressing room rehashing the material, discussing what worked and what didn't work, one of the Slate Brothers came in. The brothers wanted to extend Jackie's contract.

"How long?" asked Chartoff.

"Six months."

"We'll have to think about it."

They called Charlie Rapp in New York and he advised against it. If Jackie's that great, there should be raises and he shouldn't be tied down for that long. You never know what'll happen.

After the first night, the club was a little more crowded. By the third night, they were turning people away. Jackie was growing more and more confident. He signed a three-month contract and expanded his material. It was 1962, the season of the space race and astronauts had become a hot topic:

"Do you know why you never see a Jew in space? Because a Jew can't get out of the house. How's he gonna go into space? He can't even get out to buy a newspaper. He has to account for every minute. First of all, what Jew is gonna be able to go into space without his wife? As soon as you have a trip with any excitement to it, she wants to know, why is she left out! She'll tell him right away, 'What, you're gonna go into space without me! Who the hell are you to go there without me?'

"You wanna go to a coal mine without her you got no problem. If you're gonna go into space it sounds exotic and interesting. Right away she wants to know why she isn't included. ' 'Cause they're only letting one person go.' 'Who says so? They think I'm stupid? Every time you go someplace interesting, you tell me there's only room for one person. Why is it only one person? A spaceship costs nine million dollars. Can't they put in another chair? How much is a chair? A dollar and a quarter? I'll bring my own chair. I can bring a folding chair. It won't even take up any space. Who the hell are you bullshitting that I can't go with you? And what the hell's the reason to go there altogether. You're telling me there's nobody up there. There must be plenty of broads otherwise you wouldn't be volunteering for trips. You think you're bullshitting me? Maybe there was nobody there before but now there must be somebody there, otherwise you wouldn't be going. And what's so important about going there altogether? Why would they pick you? What, you have such a great sense of direction? I went with you to the mountains, you got lost on every trip.' "

When something really clicks, you can hear all the gears meshing, you can detect an atmospheric change. Suddenly, the Slate Brothers' club was not only packed with civilians, but there were celebrities in the house. And scouts. Three shows a night and Jackie never got tired. This was not the Golden Nights in Miami and these were not doomed housewives out there in the Danish modern darkness. There were celebrities out front — Rock Hudson, Red Buttons, Phil Silvers — and that helped keep the energy high. The master of ceremonies came out, introduced Jackie and out he came, in his business suit, looking like an accountant with sloping shoulders and bags under his eyes. Then saying the most outlandish things:

"You wanna know what's wrong with this country? The richest country in the world and we still can't show a profit. For almost two hundred years, this country has been run by Gentiles and they haven't had one successful season. Always in the red. You get a Jew in the White House, Bing! He'll show a profit."

Bill Dana was the head writer for "The Steve Allen Show." It was his custom to graze through the small clubs in the area, hunting for material and sometimes looking for talent for the show. When he looked at Jackie Mason, he recognized talent.

It didn't occur to me that I'll go on television. All I was thinking was, Maybe I'll do better. In a year, maybe, who knows. But the thought that somebody's going to put me on television that fact did not enter my mind. Maybe it started to enter my mind as a possibility, but it didn't develop into a concrete ambition. It was maybe germinating in my mind. But one night Bill Dana came into the club and he saw me and another night Jan Murray came into the club

and he saw me and he got excited. Jan Murray, at
the time, was a very hot commodity on television.
He had a show called "Treasure Hunt" and he was
considered a major personality. So he told Steve Allen, because he was a big friend of Steve Allen, and
Bill Dana told Steve Allen and he was Steve Allen's
chief writer, and all of a sudden, from all sides, he's
hearing about this new comedian who should be on
his show.

One day, I come into work and there's a call. Some
guy from "The Steve Allen Show." He says that Steve
Allen heard from a lot of people how hilarious I was
and he wants that I should come in and audition for
the show.

I hung up the phone and I remember sitting there
in a state of shock. You stand up on a stage and face
a few people. A hundred, maybe two hundred, three
hundred people. But to be on television! Who has the
nerve to face all of America? I'm just starting to feel
comfortable in a nightclub and I'm just starting to
feel impressed with myself, thinking I'm talking to
eight people at a time. All of a sudden, I'm gonna
talk to a country. This is a big step from eight people
to a country. Wait a second, let me think this over.

*The customers were starting to fill up the seats of the
Slate Brothers' club and Jackie sat by the phone, stunned
and paralyzed by the onrush of events. He was thinking about the continuity of jokes that he would need.
Before, it had been a chaos of material. What worked
fit in here. He would begin something and if it didn't
seem to be panning out, he would leave it. You couldn't
do that on television. You were committed. From the*

second you began until the second you left, it was a
long leap off a very high diving board — there was no
turning back. He would have to do something that he
had resisted — structure an act. A beginning. A middle.
And an end. The first thing he did, when he got control
of himself, was to call Bobby Chartoff. He told him
what had happened and Chartoff cooled him down.
"It's only an audition," he said.

No, I knew that it was something more. I could
feel the tingle of something much bigger than an audition. I was starting to get very excited. My life had
taken a turn. I didn't know exactly how, but I knew
something very important had happened, that I was
being given a big opportunity.

I decided, I better not think too much about it. If
I think too much about it I'll get nervous and if I get
nervous I won't be able to perform. So I didn't think
about it.

CHAPTER NINE

Jacob's Ladder

As usual, he called his brothers and there was a cross-country conference. Should he change any of his material? After all, this was television.

Family councils were called. Urgent meetings were held. Discussions became heated. The whole thing became a question with Talmudic dimensions. It evoked the nature of quality itself, ethics — all were raised and dealt with by the brothers. In New York, the brothers all stood clustered around the phone, offering long-distance opinions and commentary. Show-business Gomorrah and Mishna. Bernie said the material should remain the same since good material remained good material. Gabe was not so sure. Maybe television had its own norms of good and bad. Something that was good on a stage might not play on a small screen.

Joseph, as usual, said it was of a small consequence. Jackie would make up his own mind.

He had a point, Jackie listened, sifted, decided for himself. But he paid his respects to his brothers by listening. His sisters all had opinions, but they were not *offered. They just wished him well and said they would think of him.*

The audition turned out to be a formality. Steve Allen and a few members of his staff piled into a large conference room. There was a long wooden table and lots of chairs and the expensive teak decor of commerce. It seemed as if they were settling down for an informal business meeting. No neckties. Except for Jackie, who wore his usual stage business suit. He came in looking like he was attending his own execution, but that was just his usual baleful expression. He was, in spite of the great stakes, "comfortable." He was confident. Whatever butterflies he woke up with were gone.

And it looked like a loose, friendly audience. The staff carried coffee in plastic containers. And they kept reassuring Jackie that he was among friends. Steve Allen was clearly in charge and he set the tone for the audition. And the atmosphere was benign.

"I keep hearing about you," he told Jackie.

"So, what do you hear? Am I doing good?"

Steve Allen slapped the table. He was a sucker for another comedian.

With the ice broken, Jackie went into his act:

"Hello. How do you do. It's a pleasure for you to see me tonight. Comedians like me don't grow on trees, they swing from them. I come from the Lower East Side of New York. I had to mention this because from the way that I talk, people seem to think that I come from Alabama. Watch me carefully because I start slow but, little by little, I die out completely. It was a trick that took me years to develop. There was a time I used to stink right away. You know, I was in show business years ago but I quit. This is a comeback. Just to give you an idea of how well I was doing at the time, when I quit, do you know that I was the only person who knew about it?"

By now Steve Allen and his staff were helpless with laughter. Jackie went into his psychiatry material:

"I was once very self-conscious. Do you know I was once so self-conscious that when I went to a football game and I saw the players go into a huddle, I used to think that they were talking about me."

Steve Allen stood up. Enough, he said, talking to Jackie and talking to his staff at the same time, waving his arms in the air. "This guy is great. This is hilarious. You don't have to go any further. You got the job. You're great. I love him. Happy to see you. You'll be on the show. See that he's booked."

I remember looking at him with a great feeling of relief and nervousness at the same time. "Does this mean that I am actually going to be on television?" I asked.

"Absolutely," he says.

"Really? You think the public is ready for this?"

And again he laughs and claps me on the back and he says to his people, "I love this guy!"

I can't believe it. On the other hand, I can believe it.

It was a very sudden ascent, this rocket out of "small-time" into some other show-business realm. He wasn't a big name, but he was no longer a nobody. He was a hot young rising comedy executive.

But you wouldn't know it during the day. He lived frugally because that was the habit and style he developed when he was poor. He had no use for a lot of money. He ate a certain amount of food. He slept in one bed. He had no taste for fine food or expensive wine. He lived in the nearby motel and had his regular routine. He slept late, had his breakfast of a bagel and coffee, read the newspapers, then went out walking. In all the towns he played, he went walking.

It's a good way to see things. You see how people live. You see how they get along, how they don't get along. You can't see from a car — you're driving by too fast and you have to pay attention to the road if you're behind the wheel.

But if you're walking, you see a couple holding hands or having a fight. You see a mother talking to a child, asking if the child did his homework. You see an old man sitting on a porch watching me watching him. He's doing the same thing I'm doing only he doesn't have to work as hard. I see him and we both smile because we know right away what's what.

It's not a bad life, this living on the road, walking around the world. In New York, people don't say hello, even if they pass each other every day for twenty years. They're afraid to show an interest because they're afraid it might lead to a friendship, or to a suggestion of friendship or involvement and they'd rather not be involved with anybody they don't have a reason or purpose to know and be involved with.

But in other cities, you walk out on the street and people smile and say hello, they don't have to know you. "Good morning." "Good afternoon." Things I never heard before. If a guy says hello to you in New York and you don't know him, you could have him arrested for bothering you.

Outside of New York, I never saw anybody being impolite in hotels or in restaurants. An amazing thing. When you walk on the streets of New York, you don't see a friendly smile. Strangers look at each other with an undercurrent of fear and suspicion — people avoid everyone else. But in Dallas or in Cincinnati, you ask a person for directions, and they can't do enough for you. They go out of their way. I have even had people drive me to my destination.

I love New York, but I found this life on the road not unappealing. It had certain things to recommend it. It was, in a way, much easier to live.

In Los Angeles, there were a few friends, comedians like Corbett Monica, who had the same kind of schedule and they would sit around the same kind of coffee shop and tell the same kind of stories and trade the same kind of gossip. The weather was nice. You could walk comfortably. It was freer than New York with its forbidden neighborhoods and atmosphere of high tension. The people didn't seem to be burdened by overwhelming problems. He liked the splash and sunshine in California.

And sometimes, there was a romantic interest for Jackie, who was by now thirty-two years old and unmarried. Always, in fact, there was romance, but it didn't exist in the usual way. Jackie had strict rules and

*guidelines about his involvement with women. He was
not ready for a long-term relationship. He was not prepared to handle more than one life — his own.*

*But in Los Angeles, when he was young and not yet
cynical, there was a waitress with blond hair and a fair
smile. She was sweet and innocent and young and it
wasn't too long before she fell hopelessly in love with
the ambitious comedian from New York. And, truth be
told, Jackie was moved, too, in his fashion. He doesn't
describe it that way. He shifts in his chair and clears
his throat and admits, yes, he had a feeling for this one
waitress many, many years ago.*

She was a very nice girl. Very nice. And she started
to . . . she held my hand and she looked at me in a
certain way that I knew she had very strong feelings
for me. Very strong. I can't deny that I had a certain
feeling for her, too. I can't deny that.

*And he clears his throat and shifts in his chair. Back
in those struggling days, Jackie Mason had no room for
love in his life. He was too busy breaking free of his
past and becoming someone else. And love was such a
wild and unreliable emotion. If he conceded the possibility, he would lose all control, surrender his fate to
an outside force. That, he was unwilling to do. Besides,
he'd grown up nicely without it, thank you.*

*When he was a child, living in whatever religious
military outpost that his parents occupied, the word
love was never spoken. Tradition and duty were mentioned. All day and all night, in fact, that was all Jackie
heard. A man had his duty; a woman had her duty.
You did what you were supposed to do and what you*

were supposed to do was to get married, have children, and provide for the whole brood.

But love? Love had nothing to do with it. Love was like something weak. It stole from the other business of running a family. In Jackie's home, there was love, but it was expressed obliquely, tangibly — bread you put on the table, shirts you kept clean and mended, children whose education you didn't neglect. The home was soaked in duty and tradition — byproducts of love. But love, itself, as a plain emotion? "You know the song in Fiddler on the Roof?" *asks Jackie's brother Gabe, explaining the family manner. "The husband asks his wife if she loves him and the wife, Golda, sings, 'Do I love you?' But the question is not answered. Not directly. Golda recounts how she worked and cooked and mended and after twenty-five years, how can her husband ask such a thing?"*

Love was a distraction from the meatier obligations — duty, tradition, achievement. Survival. What did it have to do with respect or honor or the personal destiny of a future star? Talmudically, love was not provable. You couldn't deliver opinions and solicit commentaries on the facts of such an emotion.

And so, as an adult, Jackie banished the word and then the fact from his life.

The girl — this nice young waitress — loved me. She wanted to make a life together. I had to put a stop to it. Fast. I told her, "Listen, I'm not able to have such a life. I'm in show business. I live on the road. I couldn't be anything to you and you couldn't be anything to me."

She looked at me and in her eyes there was a tremendous hurt and I felt very bad. But I couldn't lead her on. Tell me, was it more cruel to tell her plain than to lead her on and to walk out one day when the fires of passion cooled? Because this was what would happen. She would love me for a while, whatever that means, and I would maybe love her for a while, if there is such a thing, and then we would have a baby. When times got hard and we couldn't stand each other, I'd walk out and the baby would be left in the middle. Who would suffer? The baby. Should I, to satisfy some momentary weakness, some emotional defect on both our parts, inflict this on an innocent child? Is this fair? Is this better? Or is it better to speak out, right away, and leave no doubt about what's going to be?

And so began the cold-blooded practice of warning all the women off. He would explain his position, which sounded so reasonable and fair and clever that a person could mistake it for a brilliant come-on. And after delivering his own personal Miranda warning, after dazzling these wide-eyed innocents with the subtle beauty of his logic and the sensitivity of his seemingly brutal detachment, he would allow the girls to give him their hearts. For who could resist such a charming and forthright pale rider of the stage?

Wait a minute, hold it. What are we talking about here? A man remains a bachelor and he is suddenly a "cold-blooded brute" (these are not my words)? There were no bachelors before? I could name a few. Sherlock Holmes, for example. Some people are not cut out for marriage. This is not yet a criminal act, unless this sick maniac has his way. I like girls. I like to be with girls. I don't like to be with the same girl all the time, which is not so terrible. Nobody gets bored. Listen, I'm interested in people. I like to meet different people.

This is stupid. I don't want to discuss this anymore.

They told him he would have six minutes. A month to organize three hundred and sixty seconds of national air time. He was sifting through events and routines, trying to find the perfect combination, when he received a telegram from one of his agents in New York. "According to Bobby Chartoff, you are scheduled to appear on 'The Steve Allen Show.' We have advised Chartoff and we are sending you this telegram to advise you that it is our opinion that you should not appear on this program as you could destroy what could be a successful career. We think that you have a very bright future, you are a very funny man, but you are not ready for national television. We implore you to take speech lessons and learn the techniques of how to reach an American audience first."

It was a very long telegram. I read it and I read it again and I said to myself, "These guys are sick bastards and absolute idiots!" Then I looked at the signature. Sure enough: a Jew.

The idea that a Jew, not a Gentile, led the attack on his career was maddening. Always the Jews stood in his path. Always the same excuse: the Gentiles won't get it. It will bring on a pogrom! Always the Jews were terrified of the reaction, of inviting attention to their Jewishness. Like the Jews in World War II who went quietly to their deaths because they didn't want to make trouble. Jackie was disgusted. He showed the telegram to Bobby Chartoff and said he was going to tear it up. He told Chartoff, just take care of the business end. Fine. The business end. He was going to earn twenty-five hundred dollars for "The Steve Allen Show."

There are old tapes of the show, broadcast in 1962, Jackie's first television appearance. He looks nervous at first. But as he gets deeper and deeper into the material, the button-down man with the accent begins to look comfortable: "The reason I never got married is as soon as a Jewish woman gets married she starts handing this poor jerk bags of garbage to take out. Where does it all come from? They never eat home — it's part of the deal. She brings home garbage so this jerk can take it out. I wouldn't mind getting married, but I don't want to go into the garbage business."

I thought I flopped because I was so nervous I couldn't hear if they were laughing or not. As soon as the red light went on, I suddenly was struck by something unbelievable, that I couldn't believe I was actually on television. I was in the electric chair. I has so much tension in my body that I couldn't remember how the jokes went over, if anybody laughed or noticed. I felt I didn't go over so good.

When I got off the stage, people said, "Wonderful! Wonderful!" but I discounted that. I thought they were being polite. So, I started to call up my friends in New York, which is three hours later, and I started to tell them that I probably did bad, that my mouth was dry and I felt so weak and unbelievably nervous. I was so frightened and insecure I couldn't hear whether or not people are laughing. I called Bobby Chartoff and Bernie Weber and I said, "I think I missed."

They got the program ahead of us in California and as soon as I got off the phone crying about how bad I did, I started to get calls saying, "Hey, it was great! It's the talk of the town. It killed people." It was "killing," "killing," "killing." Charlie Rapp called. My sisters called. A cousin. Two nephews. A friend. A relative. A friend of a friend. Everybody. And the screams over the phone were so enthusiastic that I didn't doubt the truth of it because they were like celebrating, as if, "Let's take out the champagne, you made it!"

I started to think, "My God, I'm a hit!"

Alone in Los Angeles, Jackie decided to celebrate. He took a walk. It cleared his head and put things in perspective. The long years had paid off. Now he was going to be famous, a name, playing the best hotels. He didn't have to worry about getting kicked out by stingy hotel owners.

Then he had second thoughts. Maybe his friends in New York had exaggerated. They were looking at it with bias. Maybe it wasn't such a smash. Maybe his star would blink and vanish, a one-night television phenomenon. It had happened before.

But then something convinced him that his friends had been right. "The Steve Allen Show," three hours behind New York, was playing even as he carried on this debate with himself. And as he walked along the streets of Los Angeles, people began to shout at him.

"Hey! We just saw you on television. You were great!"

"There's that guy on 'Steve Allen'! Hey, you're a funny guy!"

They leaned out of cars and yelled. They smiled and pointed as he passed.

And the smiles and shouts washed away all the doubts about his performance.

CHAPTER TEN

Stuck in Second

The next day, when Jackie showed up for work, he noticed an increase in activity in the office of the club. The Slate Brothers were stuck on the phones, fending off would-be customers. The club was sold out and they were already overbooked and the offers and pleas for tickets kept pouring in. Everybody wanted to see this new young comic who stopped the show on "Steve Allen."

The Slate Brothers, themselves, were shocked by the reaction to Jackie's single appearance. They couldn't praise Jackie enough. There was a new chair and fresh fruit in his dressing room. And two weeks later, he was booked back on "The Steve Allen Show" where he was less nervous and, this time, he heard the laughs.

Suddenly, it seemed as if a dam broke.

Bobby Chartoff was on the phone. You're not gonna believe this, Jackie, but the nightclubs want you. The Copacabana. Le Bistro. All offering five thousand dollars a week.

And he thought: With the accent!

From three hundred to five thousand dollars a week. Overnight. A couple of shots on national television and he was no longer the unsalable comedian with the unacceptable accent. He had been ratified, vindicated, blessed by the healing waters of television.

Now a record company set up microphones on the stage and Jackie Mason produced his first comedy album. It was called "I'm the Greatest Comedian in the World Only Nobody Knows it Yet," and it rode up on the charts during that season of comedy albums: Shelley Berman, Mike Nichols and Elaine May, Mort Sahl, Lenny Bruce. It was a random compilation of his regular material.

"Hello, how do you do, I knew I'd be a hit tonight as soon as I walked out. I could always tell how I'm gonna do by watching the act before me. I'm not such a sensation that I could afford to follow another stiff. I did an act last week in another place where the act before me was so bad that throughout my entire act the people kept booing him. Some people even walked out on him in the middle of my act. . . . It's an amazing thing how I came all the way here from the East Side of New York to be here tonight. You know, I come from rough circumstances. I come from rough circumstances. I come from a family of fourteen children. I'll tell you how this happened. Every night before they retired, my father said, 'Do you wanna go to sleep or what?' My mother was hard of hearing and said. 'What?'

"I like to keep a clean-act show. People are stupid. They think children are going to learn something from hearing about sex from grownups. Ridiculous. A child only learns something from other children. Did you notice that every child in the world only plays doctor. Why don't they play accountant? Even the children who want to become lawyers play doctor."

What people enjoyed were not the routines — there were very few routines — it was the person. They liked Jackie, who still did not like the structure of set routines. He preferred to ad lib his way through an evening, a kind of stream of conscious comedy.

But the record sold, despite such wheezy old jokes as "I was so ugly as a baby that my mother diapered my face." Or: "Three out of four women don't know how to express love. But that fourth woman!" "A psychiatrist told me that I love my galoshes. That's stupid. I like my galoshes."

The shows were popular, the album sold, the offers came.

I was never the type of person to jump through hoops when I was happy. I thought it was great. I was excited. But my behavior didn't change. The nice part was that my sanity was reaffirmed. I wasn't crazy. It's like the guy who says he can put up a building and another guy says you can't. Then, when you put it up and take a look, when you're finished and it's a big hit, it's a great sense of relief. In my family, I was a second-class citizen compared to my brothers, struggling to prove he's somebody so that the people in his life can respect him because, together with the fact that I was neglected as a kid, I also felt stupid compared to my brothers.

I was the guy who was not gonna amount to anything because I'm not gonna be a rabbi. What will I be? I'll be a comedian. But will it ever amount to anything? So I had an image of a flounderer who was uncertain about where to go and what to do with his life. All of a sudden, I had a sense of purpose and direction. A sense of acceptance, a sense of accomplishment, a sense that I'm somebody people respect and look up to, it vindicates me in my own mind. I don't have to worry about making a living.

He thought of his dead father. What would the learned rabbi think of the television appearances, the comedy album, and the nightclub dates? What would be his opinion of the widespread acclaim and the adulation? Jackie had always insisted that comedy was a hobby, a hiatus from his real work, a rabbi, to which he intended to return any minute.

His father would be appalled.

"My God, if he was alive, how would I hide this from him!"

It was a rare and unpleasant thought. Somehow, Jackie had managed to avoid thinking about what he was doing, in terms of his father and his father's opinion.

On my father's terms, I was a worthless person who was displaying himself, a transgressor living a worthless terrible life. So I avoided thinking about my father because it filled me with guilt. Now and then, I found myself thinking, but I would change the subject in my head. I would find a way not to think about it. It's like people who know they're gonna die, but they don't think about death. As you get older, you know that soon, it's not that long. The point is that people avoid things they can't deal with.

Now a psychiatrist could say that it's on your sub-conscious mind and that your way of dealing with it is not dealing with it and therefore you're avoiding it without knowing it, but meanwhile this guy is suc-cessfully avoiding the subject in his own conscious mind. What a psychiatrist would say on different levels is beside the point. The point is that on the conscious level, he's not thinking about it.

There was, throughout, as he traveled back and forth making the club dates from Boston to California, the soap opera called Jackie's Family. When he was near New York, he never failed to make a Friday dinner at Gabe's or Bernie's. The brothers, all rabbis and edu-cators in the New York area, always welcomed him at their tables. He needed an anchor, a vestige of lost tra-dition. The family, itself, was always in some kind of turmoil. There were plots and subplots, alliances and treachery, schemes and feuds and squabbling — in short, a mess, like all family melodrama. Someone is driving someone else crazy. Someone is teetering back and forth, thinking of getting a divorce. Shames and scandals are stifled and smothered. But, still, within that turbulent structure, there was always a fierce attachment. Jackie came to dinner on Friday nights. He loved the soap opera.

And the brothers came to see him wherever he played. They were stern and steady supporters and sometimes the sight of them there, was heartbreaking and touch-ing, these orthodox Jewish men in their awkward felt hats and stone faces, sitting bolt upright in the dining room of Sardi's (looking as if they were afraid that they were about to be assaulted by a piece of nonkosher food) among the glitzy, unrestrained crowd of show-business lights and satellites. They were family sentries, giving their consent to Jackie's career by their very presence.

Now that he had some money, some stature in the community, some professional recognition, Jackie assumed the role of family patriarch. He set up one sister's husband in a cleaning store, he opened a kosher deli for another and, when that failed, a real estate office. He rented an apartment for his mother in Forest Hills, a trendy section of Queens, where she was not the rabbi's wife, she was Jackie Mason's mother.

He bought everyone in the family television sets. He sent two hundred dollars a week home for expenses.

He planted seed money for his nephews' education. He sat back and watched the fame affect his brothers' attitude toward him. He was no longer the hopeless dreamer who had forsaken his ancestral duty for the sake of a golden calf. He was a shining light, admired and quoted in the streets. People solicited his autograph!

It was not possible for the members of the family — even the brothers who regarded show business as vaguely sinful — to witness the great orgy of admiration and not be impressed.

I asked my mother if she watched the television shows and she said that she did. So I asked if she enjoyed it, and she said, yes, she enjoyed watching me. She said she can't believe it, that I'm actually on television. But she was troubled. I could see that something bothered her. She didn't understand what great purpose this had, this standing up on television and making wisecracks. She was a woman with a religious background. It didn't fit into any of the past experiences as far as she was concerned.

This was new and therefore dangerous. Do I really need it, because, to tell you the truth, she thought it would be a lot easier to make a living as a rabbi, it's easier to make a living without getting involved in all this, because she could see that it's a hard life, going from one city to another. Isn't it better to have a home, to have a family, isn't it better to be married and have children? That's what she felt.

Still, she got a kick out of me. Whenever I came home, she got joy in seeing me. And soon she stopped saying things that weren't gonna get an answer. She accepted. She made the best of things. As long as I was happy. As long as I was making a living. As long as I had enough to eat.

It was during this first burst of success that Jackie paid for his mother's trip to Israel. She went with one of her daughters and one night, in a Tel Aviv hotel room, she died of a heart attack.

Jackie was off on a club date when it happened. He thinks he was in Toronto at the time. But he's not positive. He doesn't remember too clearly because he has this ability to shut out what he doesn't want to remember.

But if it was Toronto or Detroit, it doesn't make much difference. He refused to attend his mother's funeral. It was that same mental quirk: if he didn't see it, maybe it didn't happen.

But when he heard about his mother's death, not even he was strong-minded enough to change the subject.

He could not forget her great sustaining force, when she kept his father away, when she made certain that he had enough to eat, when she stood between Jackie and all the people who wanted him to submit, to give in. It didn't matter to her that Jackie was impious. It didn't matter that he defied tradition. Hers was a love unqualified. Hers was, after all, the single, largest source of felt love in his life. Alone, in a hotel room in a strange, forgotten city, he wept for his dead mother.

The nightclub bookings kept him busy. He went from one city to another — Philadelphia, Dallas, Cincinnati, Columbus, Ohio. In Chicago, he played Mister Kelley's, amid the false brick and summer iconoclasts. He detected the odor of marijuana backstage, but he was never even tempted by liquor or drugs. He was too concerned with keeping his wits. In New York, he played the Copacabana and the gangsters and ballplayers doubled up as much as the Chicago beatniks. He was playing nightclubs and making star appearances on "The Jack Paar Show," a late-night talk show whose host was emotionally volatile and had great affections for Jackie Mason.

Jack Paar liked the sound of my voice. A Gentile never heard a person talk like this before. I could see in his eyes that he enjoyed whatever it was that I was saying and he always wanted me back. He had a talk show and he would have me on and I would do my act and then I would come and sit down and talk some more and he would sit there smiling. He smiled and smiled and he always asked me back.

The material began to worry him. Now that he was making a lot of television appearances, he needed fresh jokes. He carried a pencil and a notepad and he wrote down ideas. He sampled his friends. He polled everyone. What's on your mind? What do you think of the state of the world? Who's popular? He worked small clubs in Brooklyn, to try out material — little dens that changed their names every week — The Sand, The Silver Cloud — where young hoodlums and their flashy dates co-opted the front tables. Sometimes the material landed with a thud, but that was all right, too. He learned from his mistakes. "I can always spot a hooker. Let me ask you, mister, is that lady a hooker?" The Italians bristled. An insult to their women — even one that was clearly a joke — was unacceptable. Jews didn't mind. But Mediterranean tempers flared when you spoke of their wives, "the madonna."

Finally, Jackie landed a spot on "The Ed Sullivan Show," the diamond showcase of the variety shows. The television appearances kept his name up high, but the bread and butter was still out on tour. He still had to crisscross the country, showing the flag, as it were. He was comfortable in his role as a stranger and sojourner in the land. But he wasn't always allowed to maintain his preferred distance. He couldn't always watch unmolested.

I would go to a town, say Des Moines. And the Jews would come to see the show and they would feel a certain natural degree of excitement about my appearance. They would feel a special fraternity because Jews in far-off places have to stick together, because they feel like a beleaguered minority. They would feel like they have to stick together to survive. When you went to the small towns you would find that most of the Jews, regardless of how much they tell you how comfortable they are with the Gentiles, when you start questioning them, you'll find that their closest friends are Jews. There is an undercurrent of separatism.

Sometimes, in the beginning, I would accept an invitation to their homes. But this is a big mistake. I never felt comfortable in somebody else's home. I became like a prisoner. You come to somebody's home you have to respect his presence in his own home, you have to adhere to his behavior, you have to sit at his table and listen to some of the stupidest opinions and the worst conversation you ever heard. After five minutes, I would have a vicious headache. You're a prisoner because he's giving you a meal. Once you get in there, you can't get out. And then they take out the pictures. "This is my aunt when she was two; she was a beauty. You can't tell from this picture. This is Uncle Harold. You can't tell from this picture, but he looked the spitting image of Robert Redford." Everybody was handsome and gorgeous, only they didn't happen to have these particular pictures. They only had the ones where they looked miserable and ugly. I never understood why people would want to burden you with the record and chronology of their families. Their backgrounds. Their accomplishments.

It wasn't only ordinary people. There was a night I made a mistake and went to dinner at the home of Rudy Vallee in Beverly Hills. It was the most miserable experience I ever had in my life. He had a big, big, old house, worth millions. And he had closets and closets of memorabilia. He had every kind of memorabilia. If he worked someplace, he had a picture of a building. If he saw a show, he had a picture of the lobby. I kept saying, "Fantastic!" "No kidding?" "How do you like that!" By the time I got out of that house I was so miserable and nauseous, I couldn't believe it. The man was living in the past, reliving everything through you. It's a constant source of amazement to me that people will bore you to death with their own sick egos.

No, he preferred the coffee shops or restaurants where you can get up and walk out if you don't like the food or the company. Better not to be tied down to innocent vanity and small talk. True to his own credo, Jackie preferred to be alone on the road. Except for the ever-changing female friends who were like cut flowers at his table. And there was always someone putting fresh flowers at his table. The women sent notes, called his room, waited like stage-door Johnnies outside of the clubs to approach him. There was something appealing and cute about him that turned out to be seductive.

But the road did not quite live up to his expectations, as far as his career was concerned. Even with his television exposure.

In many cases, I did very little business. The nightclub owners were surprised because they saw me on "Paar" and on "Ed Sullivan" and they thought this is a sensation. I had a name. Not a big name, but a name that they thought should draw a few people. I was supposed to be hot. They were paying me five, six thousand a week and they're losing money. They think I'm gonna pack the house and this is not the way it's turning out. I couldn't figure out why. They couldn't figure out why. It's just some performers pull a certain amount and that's it. It could change. Something happens and the public changes its mind. But why? Nobody knows.

Meanwhile, I'm coming down to Miami Beach in the winter and playing the Catskills in the summer. There is a guy who keeps coming to see me, wherever I'm playing in the mountains. Jack Roy. This is his real name. He changed it now to Rodney Dangerfield. A very nervous man. But he comes to see me, every show, and he can't stop telling me what a genius I am. I'm the best, I'm brilliant, I'm a genius. He idolized me. And he tells me that he's miserable because he can't perform his own material. "You're so lucky," he says, "because you can tell jokes. Me, I can write jokes, but I can't tell them. I don't have any particular personality or style. When I tell a joke, the joke has to be perfect. But you're funnier than any joke."

He, himself, did not know that he had a colorful, comedic personality because he used to tell jokes in a simple style. He didn't have the nervous twitches yet. This is before he came up with "no respect."

He follows me around the mountains, he follows me in the city and while we're sitting around in a coffee shop and he offers to write me some jokes. So, I pay him seven hundred and fifty dollars — one of the few efforts I ever actually made to hire a writer. And the jokes were good. I couldn't use them, but

they were good. They weren't my style. They were
his style. He would say, for example, that his wife is
so ugly that she scares the dog. And he doesn't have
a dog. My style is less blunt. I wouldn't go for that
direct, brutal kind of laugh. I would try to make the
joke on me, or on the situation, but not on another
person.

But he needed the cash — you had to pay him in
cash — and I was looking for material because I'm
so busy, so I paid him and he wrote some things
for me.

It's funny. When he started to do his own material, when he started to click, he didn't want to know
me. He forgot that I was a genius and brilliant and
he was nobody. He would walk up to the Carnegie
Deli and look in the window to see if I'm there. He
doesn't want to bump into me. This same man who
chased me around the mountains.

*It is a fickle and mind-altering state, celebrity. It iso-
lates a person from a normal context. You begin to
think that you are always being noticed. Always on
display. That your presence is being recorded in some
mysterious and permanent fashion. You can't look
around, because it is unseemly, so as you go through
life with your head fixed, staring straight ahead, and
you assume all eyes are on your passage. You miss a
lot when you are a celebrity. The distortion is sudden
and not often understood, but Jackie saw it clearly.*

*Once, coming off the road, Jackie Mason shared a
cab from La Guardia Airport with Max Lerner, a famous newspaper columnist and admired intellectual.
Jackie prattled on about how much he respected Max*

Lerner, how he read every column, how proud he was of the liberal banner that Max Lerner held high. They rode into town and Jackie would not let Max Lerner pay his half of the fare. A tribute from a fan.

About two years later, I'm in London watching a play and I see him again. I run over to him and I say, "Remember me?" He looks blank. He never heard of me. I just made a shmuck out of myself.

Not so different from the guy in Miami who took Jackie around his house, showing him pictures of the woulda-been-coulda-been actress who was his daughter. Not so different from the late Rudy Vallee holding up a plaque given to him by some obscure club in some remote town. Not so different from Rodney Dangerfield running away from the Carnegie Deli because he seemed to be afraid Jackie was going to dim his own light.

CHAPTER ELEVEN

A Show-Business Curse

I arrived in Detroit it was maybe six o'clock in the evening. The club was called Dinty's and it was a good room. The sound was good. The tables were arranged so that the waiters didn't bang into each other and make a racket when they served the customers. And as long as the lights were down, you couldn't tell that the furnishings were getting a little old. But any club, if you turned up the lights, you saw things that you didn't want to see. Tears in the artificial leather seats. Holes in the walls. Some dead insects on the floor. You didn't want to look too close or see too much. I saw what I had to see and for an entertainer, it was a good room.

I had a habit, I would get into town and immediately go over to the club to check out the room and the owners would greet me and they would be very friendly and they would try to cheer me up. "Business is picking up! A lot of calls."

But I sensed that business wasn't so hot. Most of the time the owners were gracious and they'd tell me,

"Don't worry, people are coming in, it's getting better." Or else they'd have an excuse: "It rained yesterday"; "It's two weeks before Thanksgiving"; "Nobody likes to come out when it's Christmas." Four o'clock in the morning they're shopping. They're shopping, they're shopping. No stores are open, but they're shopping.

And the weather was always something.

"But the weather's good."

"Yeah, now, but it's gonna get worse."

A waiter would say it's going to be a great crowd. A busboy would say, Don't worry, things are going to pick up.

And the boss would be nice, couldn't be nicer. They always treated me with the courtesy and respect due a star. When a star is not doing great business, he's still a star. And the boss still feels he has to show some respect because I'm on television and that makes me a star.

The performances themselves were professional and polished. Jackie had tapes and notebooks full of material. He didn't have a set strategy, just an idea of where he would go and what he would do. He would start with his family and go into the psychiatrist. He made a reference to something local if it was relevant. An election. A big strike. And then he went into his army routine:

"They wanted to draft me in the army and I went down to take the physical. They called me in to talk to the psychiatrist and I said, 'Show me those Germans, I'll kill them, I'll slaughter them, I don't need any help, I'll do it alone.'

"He said, 'You're crazy!'

"I said, 'Write it down!'

"Listen, I don't mind serving my country; I'm proud to fight for my country. But what a ridiculous time to call me, during a war!"

Maybe the people who came into nightclubs in the early '60s demanded something bluer, material with more anger and sex than they got on television. Whatever the reason, Jackie didn't pack the nightclubs, but he was still a sensation on television. For whatever reason, the public who didn't flock to see him personally, watched him on TV. (Ironically, he became their prisoner anyway. They brought him into their living rooms on their television sets.)

I don't understand all this worry and censorship about sex. Children are not supposed to see sex. Violence is all right but sex, no. It doesn't make any sense. A child won't know what he's looking at if he sees sex. He thinks it's a fight. Two people, sweating and wrestling. Suddenly, he's knocked out and she's dancing. How did a little thing like this woman knock out this big strong guy? He didn't even see the punch. It's ridiculous!

Nevertheless, even when he played to a near-empty house, Jackie was always a surprise hit. The people who came to see him began howling from the minute he started in until they were left limp with laughter. He didn't attract hecklers. His fans were usually couples, usually married, usually well dressed.

I just wasn't that big a draw. Some guys aren't. I was never on the level of a Jerry Lewis, Alan King, or a Buddy Hackett. I'd be willing to bet that two-thirds of the nightclub owners were disappointed in the amount of business that people like me brought in.

Reasons I don't know. I go to Atlantic City or play Las Vegas and I bring down the house. Always liked to play in towns where there is gambling. There is a different atmosphere. Festive. Whether they win or lose, it makes no difference. People go to have a good time and they have no troubles on their mind. They're in a better frame of mind. They don't even mind losing money in the gambling.

A guy loses ten thousand dollars, he's looking for a place to have a laugh. They don't feel half as bad as the person who hears about it. They laugh more when they lose. It's not so strange because they need to forget the losing and they are out for a good time to begin with so you can get a lot of laughs from bad gamblers. Maybe there's something masochistic in gamblers, I don't know.

Why did I do good at the Desert Inn and the Aladdin in Las Vegas and bad in Dinty's Detroit? Could not understand it. I was still making good money. Not like Tony Bennett. Entertainers like Tony Bennett could pick up seventy, eighty thousand dollars a week, while I was getting eighty-five hundred a week, tops ten thousand.

But I knew that I was funny. I just was not packing the house. What was the secret? I could not figure this out, although, who was I to complain? I was not living a bad life at the time. There wasn't much I needed. I would go to Toronto where I would appear at the Royal York Hotel and I would wander the streets of the city, which I liked very much, but I would not do much business in Toronto. For some reason, I couldn't fill a house. But, I enjoyed myself, because it's a very cosmopolitan city, a busy city and there are a lot of things to do and a lot of neighborhoods and the people have a smile on their face, not like the misery you see on the faces in New York. They don't knock you over the head for a dime. They don't push you out of the way for a taxi.

Or I would go to Columbus, Ohio, where they never even saw a Jew, and I remember asking somebody in a coffee shop how to get to a certain place and this man put me in his car and drove me there. He went out of his way, but he thought nothing of it, that's the way they are.

Texas. I happen to like Texas. Would you believe that in Texas, people couldn't be nicer. Everything was "Please" and "Thank you" and "Would you mind." Such manners and politeness! Why this didn't translate into business, I couldn't understand. If they were so polite, why didn't they come to see the show?

It was during this fragile period in his career — a moment when a small trickle of doubt began to erode his confidence — that he had his famous encounter with Ed Sullivan. On that night, October 18, 1964, two

*headstrong men with hairtrigger personalities were on
a collision course.*

*Jackie might have taken the optimist's position, that
the furor could rain down publicity benefits, bring him
to the attention of that crossover audience who had
resisted him, who would not come out to see him, but
the truth was much more bleak.*

*The reality was that he left a lasting impression of
bad taste in the public's mind. On a word-association
test, Jackie Mason would conjure up smutty unreliabil-
ity. This might be all right for someone like Joe E. Lewis,
but for a former clergyman, it was unforgivable.*

I don't remember the Sullivan show having any
specific impact on my drawing power or my stardom
except for the fact that it had an impact on my future stardom. I think that whatever interest there might
have been for big things for me immediately evapo-
rated even though the interest in any big things wasn't
appreciably there anyway. I was being considered, I
was recommended, but in the end it was always too
Jewish. Now they had an excuse and they said "This
is a neurotic, unpredictable sick guy who could do
something so disgusting on television, this is the guy
that made the filthy gesture." Nobody even doubted
that I was guilty, that I made a filthy gesture. Once
Sullivan announced the filthy gesture, they assumed it.

*By winter it was clear that Jackie's career had taken
a nose dive. The Americana Hotel canceled a two-week
engagement. Bobby Chartoff was spending half his time
explaining, apologizing, reassuring the booking agents
and club owners.*

To little avail. Jackie's price fell like a bad stock. He was still headlining the Concord on Saturday night for twenty-five hundred dollars, but other bookings were not so easy to get and the asking price was dropping.

There were crisis meetings with his brothers in which they all sat down — one big brooding clan — and tried to figure out what had happened to Jackie. Bernie thought that it was bad, very bad, and that Jackie would suffer the consequences of the public perception that he had sinned. Because you were a rabbi, said Gabe, you are held to a higher moral standard. A rabbi must behave above reproach.

Joseph sat silent.

Jackie held up a hand. "Wait a minute. I'm innocent! I didn't do anything!"

Well, whether you did or you didn't, it's what people believe, said Bernie.

All night long, every night, miserable and depressed, the family sat and debated and argued and complained.

See, this is what happens when you go into show business!

What has going into show business got to do with it?

It's not a serious business!

Underneath, this is what all the brothers believed. Jackie was engaged in a business that was not serious. That meant that the audience was fickle. They did not take a person seriously. They would desert at the first sign of trouble.

They were generous in the mountains. They still loved Jackie. But in the clubs, every once in a while, a new note appeared. Someone would yell something. Pig! Vulgar bastard! And Jackie would go back to his dress-

ing room afterward, shaken, that this thing with Ed
Sullivan had such a long life.

Everyone says that I have to go on the offensive.
This vicious lie is ruining me. And I can't seem to
catch up with it. Everybody believes it. So I hired a
lawyer, Paul O'Dwyer, because we were friends and
we agreed on many issues, and because he was the
best, and we took out a lawsuit.

Manhattan City Councilman Paul O'Dwyer, with his
long mane of white hair and his thick Irish brogue, was
one of those secular saints who seem to enter public
life to remind us that there are unselfish people who
come along now and then. All his causes were en-
hanced by a kind of unmistakable aura of virtue — de-
spite the fact that his brother left the mayoralty of New
York City in disgrace. If you wanted to determine who
was the bully in any specific dispute, it was the side
against which Paul O'Dwyer fought. Paul O'Dwyer was
a powerful advocate of the Irish Republican Army and
through that connection came to be a friend of Israel.
When Bernie Weber, Bushee, got into trouble for alleg-
edly helping run guns to the infant state in 1948, he
was defended by Paul O'Dwyer. When Jackie was
looking for a lawyer, Bushee recommended O'Dwyer.
O'Dwyer had championed civil rights, he championed
tenants against landlords, and he championed Jackie
Mason. On February 23rd, 1965, O'Dwyer filed a three-
million-dollar damage suit in the New York Supreme
Court against Ed Sullivan.
Legally, it looked bad for Sullivan. After one prelim-
inary hearing, a judge refused to throw out the charges,

*claiming that, having viewed the tapes, he could find
nothing vulgar in Jackie Mason's performance. But that
was legally a technicality, and it didn't hold much water
with the public who had a fixed, hard opinion about
who was right and who was wrong when it came to
Jackie Mason and Ed Sullivan.*

*On April 2, 1965, Broadway gossip columnist Earl
Wilson tried to make peace between Jackie Mason and
Ed Sullivan. He used his syndicated column as a forum,
using a lot of Jackie's material:*

So hear ye! . . . I appeal once more to Ed Sullivan
and Jackie (Goldfinger) Mason, the comedian, to make
up. I wish Mason'd drop that $3,000,000 law suit
against Ed. . . . I wish Ed would take Jackie back,
finger and all. . . . I feel that Jackie's satirical commentary about Our Leaders is needed today.

A disappointingly small audience saw Jackie open at
Basin St. E — I kept feeling that if he had his old status
with Ed he'd have packed it.

"Why did they fire Bobby Baker?!" he [Jackie] demanded. "They should have made him a partner! The
only guy working for the government that ever showed
a profit. . . . Imagine if he could have adver-
tised. . . .

"Goldwater could have won but his timing was
wrong. He ran at the beginning of November — just
when Johnson was running.

"Nixon gets bigger — he's a professional loser. He
knows his business. I'd like to see him run against Ad-
lai Stevenson. Nobody would win.

"And I'm for economy. What do they mean spending
$12 for a bottle of champagne to christen a battleship?

If I was President, I wouldn't christen a battleship. I'd bar-mitzvah it. Instead of champagne, they'd use a glass of tea. Not only that — everyone would give a gift besides."

He also said Mayor Wagner "is doing very well — for himself."

Jackie, introduced as "Ed Sullivan's favorite comedian," said, "Ed doesn't hate me, he really loves me, he just doesn't know it."

Jackie's topper was: "Ask in any country, 'Where's the American Embassy?' They'll tell you, 'Oh, it's just a stone's throw away.' "

Even with the blurring of time, it is possible to hear Jackie's voice and guess at the meaning of the jokes he delivered to the empty house at Basin Street East. Even if you don't know that Bobby Baker was a corrupt official in the Johnson administration and that Goldwater got creamed by Johnson in the '64 election, the jokes are still funny. Jackie still didn't like political humor, but in New York, people wanted to hear liberal commentary. It was the era of Mort Sahl and bitter satire and once in a while, Jackie gave in and delivered some political jokes. Basically, his humor was still social, not political. He would never feel entirely comfortable delivering strict political messages. But in his desperation to be accepted back into New York/Broadway favor, he was willing to try.

Earl Wilson notwithstanding, it didn't help. Ed Sullivan's accusation hung over Jackie's career like a curse.

Now began the frantic years, when he would flounder and search for redemption.

CHAPTER TWELVE

High Jinx

I have been blessed with the ability to forget just about everything. I can look back at my life and see only the things that I want to see. I mean, I know there was poverty and suffering in my youth. I know that there was a long period of misery after the Sullivan show. But, fortunately, it is a blur. I remember it as if it happened to somebody else. In a sense, it did.

Before he became a best-selling author, Robert Ludlum was in the theater. First as an actor, then as a producer and director. In late April of 1965, Ludlum, who was then thirty-eight years old, was producing and directing a British comedy written by Bernard Kops, called Enter Solly Gold, *at Playhouse on the Mall in Paramus, New Jersey. The play, which had a successful run in London, was scheduled to work out the crimps in New Jersey, then, once the actors got their stage legs, cross the Hudson River to Broadway. Jackie was to play the lead, the part of a con man.*

The play opened April 23, 1965, a Thursday, and rather than being a night of high comedy and music, it had the ring of a great tragedy. At intermission, almost half the audience left and never came back. The critics, unfortunately, returned and finished off the play.

There was a feeling of gloom around the theater the next day, but Ludlum was a trooper. We'll have to get to work and put the thing back together, he said. Learn our lines. Come in better on cues. He was looking at Jackie who had a habit of wandering off on improvised sprays of humor. It was funny for the audience, but the other actors were thrown badly. They were waiting for the cues while Jackie did comedy routines. Ludlum spent eight grueling hours putting the actors through a punishing rehearsal. He insisted that Jackie recite the lines as written, rather than improvise.

Thus, he set the stage for a memorable final act.

My feeling is that nobody knew what they were doing. I know comedy. I had an idea of what an audience likes and doesn't like. To be so wed to the lines of a script — I didn't believe that this was the way to get the best out of this play.

Besides, after the whole day of rehearsing on Friday, I was very tired. A whole day of rehearsing and then to go out on the stage, very tiring. Two days' work in one.

The members of the cast sensed a dangerous stubble of insubordination on Jackie's face. He was obedient to the script . . . but with a man of his volatility, who knows.

"He was very good," recalled Ludlum, who was to be transformed by this collaboration with Jackie. "His performance on the Friday was infinitely better than Thursday's. It showed after his all-day rehearsal, as the audience reacted with hilarity to his treatment of the lines. It was so much better and different from the night before. He kept the audience in hysterics most of the night."

This was true, up to a point. Jackie was not finished. There was still one final piece of business before the curtain. The con man (Jackie) is supposed to turn gooey and sympathetic at the end, and this was the sore point between actor and producer.

In other words, it was supposed to be a serious moment, something for which Jackie was not prepared. He comes out onto the stage with a suitcase, sits on it and is supposed to sing "Work is for the Working Class, But Not for Solly Gold."

Not for Jackie either. He sat down on the suitcase, shook his head, got up, picked up the suitcase and marched to the footlights — breaking down the fourth wall of the theater before such stagecraft was chic — and told the audience that he could not go any further.

Ludlum groaned. (One of the nicer pieces of fallout from this odd bit of behavior was that Ludlum quit producing shows and turned to producing best-selling books — The Scarlatti Inheritance, The Holcroft Covenant, The Bourne Identity, The Parsifal Mosaic, *among others.)*

Jackie held up his hands, quieting the audience. "Ladies and gentlemen, the end of this play is so beautiful I don't want to louse it up."

Then he did a few jokes and walked offstage, leaving behind, as he so often would when a stage production fell apart, a trail of bewildered and confused actors and stagehands to handle the explanations and make the apologies.

Jackie was accustomed to the role of a standup comedian. He had control of the stage. If something went wrong, it was his fault. Now, however, there was an ensemble, and the notion of mutual, or shared, responsibility didn't sink in. The director, the other actors — they were not the affected parties, as far as Jackie was concerned. He, alone, bore the duty of making the play a success. There was no point discussing it; he failed. When he saw the play falling apart, it was like standing on a stage and not getting jokes during a monologue. He felt an unaccustomed panic. The form that his panic usually took was a kind of high-minded defiance.

I was lying. The ending wasn't beautiful. It was terrible. I would have said anything. I didn't want to tell the truth, which is that I didn't think that anybody there had any idea of what they were doing. I didn't think it was working.

There was, of course, the usual amused agitation by the press about madcap Jackie's latest stunt. Already, they had begun to sense the emergence of a major eccentric among the comic players of lighter news. This man seemed to have a gift for attracting lightning.

And in some dim, subtle way, Jackie seemed intent on confirming the Sullivan judgment, that he was unprofessional and unreliable. Even if that was not his intention, this gave his enemies plenty of ammunition.

Did you hear the latest about Jackie Mason? You didn't even have to hear. The eyebrows rose like a curtain on his wacky image.

Ed Sullivan was the farthest thing from my mind. I was thinking of the customers who paid money to see a show and were getting crap. What am I, an idiot, that I would destroy myself if I didn't have a good reason? This show stunk. Period. The writing was bad. The direction was lousy. I didn't feel comfortable in the part. I agree what I did was unprofessional. But is it so sacred, a play, that you cannot change a word? Is this Shakespeare? It was a lousy little play in a lousy little theater in New Jersey and I thought I could give the audience a better show if I didn't do that last song.

But, no, it wasn't the "professional" thing to do.

The press showed up, smiling already, because, after all, this wasn't a homicide or an indictment. This was a silly sidebar that was bound to be fun. It was still 1965, a time when dogs and celebrities belonged to the feature side of newspapers, long before "Entertainment Tonight" and all the other functionally worshipful television organs transformed celebrities into statesmen. Journalists still viewed society and show-business celebrities with a certain amount of disdain, even contempt.

Even as they assumed their professionally neutral pose, the tack was taken: He's done it again!

Questions were posed. Answers were demanded. The Playhouse producer, Ludlum, was a model of dignity as he mildly and publicly rebuked his star.

"In theatrical terminology, he just 'went up,' " ex-
plained Ludlum to the assembled reporters. "To 'go
up' means you just can't function. He was alone on
stage and there was no one to pull him out of it."

Ludlum explained that the long rehearsal and the
devastating reviews had taken a toll on Mason's stam-
ina. After he "went up," Ludlum said, Jackie wept and
promised that it would never happen again.

But two nights later, Jackie landed in another splashy
tabloid mess again — and it didn't matter why, the mere
appearance in another public brawl seemed to confirm
his shaky new status.

In fact, this time, he seemed to be a perfectly inno-
cent participant in this incident. He was walking along
East 53rd Street near Lexington Avenue at 2 o'clock in
the morning, after the show in New Jersey, when he
saw a man being chased by Albert Quain, headwaiter
at the Monkey Bar one block away.

The headwaiter is yelling, "Stop thief! Stop, thief!"
and he's chasing someone down the block. I am not
going to just stand there like a shmuck, not after I've
been out in America where, if you hear someone
yelling "Stop, thief!" you do something about it.
Not after I'm complaining that people don't get involved and are indifferent to each other. So I go
after this guy, too. I chase him. But I don't think
about it. If I would think about it, I'd probably call
a cop.

The sixty-year-old headwaiter fell behind, but Jackie
Mason, only thirty-two at the time, caught up with the
man at 52nd Street and Madison Avenue. He lunged

and brought him down with a flying tackle. By then, police were on the scene and they pulled Jackie off the man.

Jackie was surprised to see that his target was a well-dressed businessman. Not the sort of person you see rolling around in the gutter in the middle of the night.

Back at the Seventeenth Precinct on 51st Street, the headwaiter and bartender from the Monkey Bar were waiting. The man, who was an advertising executive from Hartford, Connecticut, had put away nine scotches, then, when presented with the bill — $15.13 — bolted for the street, which is where Jackie came in.

He had no money. He emptied his pockets to show us. He was broke. The guy was a sad case. I felt very bad for him.

Jackie gave Quain twenty dollars to cover the man's bar tab, plus a healthy tip. The he gave the advertising executive carfare back to Connecticut.

The man wanted to give me something, to show his gratitude. How do you like that? He wanted to give me his rosary beads — blessed by Pope John yet. I told him he should keep his rosary beads. I explained that I'm a former rabbi but I appreciate the thought just the same.

For the tabloids, this story was like buttermilk. It even had the exquisite Broadway, heart-of-gold ending, complete with a soft quote delivered with a side of the mouth twist. When a reporter asked him why he did it,

*why he paid the bill, Jackie replied: "Maybe I got a
kind heart."*

Damon Runyon could not have written it better.

*It was not unusual for Jackie Mason to be out walk-
ing the streets at 2 o'clock in the morning. In New
York, he'd usually be with his friend Bernie Weber,
Bushee.*

*Jackie would walk slowly admiring the buildings, his
hands behind his back. It reminded Bernie of someone:
Jackie's father, Eli. When Rabbi Maza was alive, Jackie
and he would go walking once a week. It was a ritual.
They would walk and his father would repeat over and
over, "That's a building!" and Jackie would respond,
"That's some building."*

*Walking through the streets, admiring the architec-
ture, it was one habit Jackie took from his father. He
took it across America. Wherever he went, he'd walk
the streets for hours and admire the buildings. Sometimes with Bushee. But when he was off playing clubs,
alone, he was repeating aloud, "That's some building!"
to his dead father.*

I, personally, do not believe in saving money and
I'll tell you why. Every year the value of the dollar
goes down. It's a losing proposition to save money.
On the other hand, every year the value of bread
goes up. So it makes sense to save bread, not money.
Unfortunately, I found this out too late. All my life,
I've been eating my profits.

*Jackie Mason does not know how money works. Not
in any deep, technical way. He knows that if you hand
someone a piece of paper currency you stand a good*

*chance of getting it exchanged for goods or services.
But where this flimsy piece of paper obtains its value is
a complete mystery to him. Another mystery is a check.
He has no personal understanding of the credit system.
Oh, he knows that if he borrows money, maybe somebody is out something somewhere. But his own personal role in all these transactions is as mystifying to
him as the Cabala. This is, of course, a residue of his
ascetic childhood, an enduring recognition of his father's faith and a subtle rejection of the material world.
In his life he had earned some wealth, but this was not
the measure of achievement. Not in his father's terms.
Not in his own terms. Money was useful only to the
extent that it propelled him to greater and greater heights
of show business. Somewhere up there, somewhere beyond stardom, his fame would catch up to his father's
expectations.*

*Which is why he always tried to remain shielded from
the complex world of finance. When his boyhood
friend — call him Harvey — came to him and said, Let's
start a business, Jackie said, Good, sure, let's start a
business. Sounds good.*

*And they did. Harvey contributed his knowledge of
business and Jackie put up money; he had all this sur-
plus cash from the club dates and the mountains and
Miami and Las Vegas and he sunk it into this business.
The business itself was a manufacturing concern and
for a while, it thrived. There were profits. Large profits. One year Jackie's share was a hundred thousand
dollars.*

*But suddenly, the profits began to dry up. Business
still looked good. The merchandise was moving. Harvey
was still driving around in a limousine, still putting up*

a big front, still flying to Europe to see what the competition was up to. But the partners saw no dividends.

One day, Jackie took Harvey aside and said, in essence, What gives? Where are the profits?

Harvey confessed. He was a hopeless alcoholic and had wasted all the money. Lost it gambling.

He knew how to run a business, it was his life that he couldn't run. But, he was a friend and I didn't do anything about it and I just forgot. A couple of years later, he comes to me again and says, "Let's start a business." He needed a hundred thousand dollars. I had to borrow some of it, but I gave it to him. The man needed help. Well, I don't have to tell you, I never saw a nickel back from that. Same thing.

But, you live and learn. Turns out that this man is still in bad shape and he comes to see me. He says he needs some money. I give him. He says he's looking for a job. President, vice-president.

I said, Does it have to be the boss? Why not any job?

He says, How would it look?

It was a jolt. He had seen his money squandered and he had seen Harvey's unrepentant greed. Jackie was outraged. Not that the man had a sickness or that he wanted more money. Not even that he took money that didn't belong to him. He was offended in some deep, moral way. It was a question of honor, taking responsibility for one's acts, being honest, doing something to earn the bread that you put in your mouth — values that lay at the core of those beliefs that had been hammered home in those long, painful hours of Talmudic study in the oppressive synagogue. The moral lessons clung like some ethical birthmark, shifting and adjusting in the outside world, but always there, always a factor.

CHAPTER THIRTEEN

Frank's Place

In the summer of 1966, Jackie was at the Las Vegas airport with Bernie Weber. Jackie had been working the Flamingo Hotel in Las Vegas with Redd Foxx. Jackie always got steady work in the gambling dens, working the lounges where he was a headliner. He didn't pull down the money that Wayne Newton earned in the main room, but he was a solid draw in the hotel lounges with their deep banquettes to take the sting out of losing. Sinatra and Dean Martin worked the main rooms, where waiters were forbidden to serve during their acts, but the bread and butter came from the lounges where the gamblers caught their breath between assaults on the crap table, and Jackie Mason was always popular. But it was summer and he had a rendezvous with his Catskills destiny. In the summer, a comic had to put in some time on the circuit — the Concord, Kutscher's, Grossinger's, the Raleigh. It was fine to cross America and earn money in Las Vegas, but the Catskills were something reliable, familiar, and safe. Jackie could al-

ways find work and an appreciative audience in the
Borscht Belt.

When you say appreciative, it's like saying a mob
likes a good hanging. These people who came to the
shows at the Concord came to judge you. Critics.
"He did that joke about the elevator music last year.
It was funnier." "He should use the joke about the
psychiatrist there. People always laugh at a good
psychiatrist joke." You should hear: a house full of
critics, worse than the *Times* put together.

Bernie — Bushee — was Jackie's entourage as he
headed back to New York. Bushee carried Jackie's bags
(an easy job because there were no bags, Jackie did not
believe in luggage; he bought whatever he needed
wherever he went. He left a spoor of abandoned cloth-
ing all across America). Bushee reminded Jackie of his
appointments, which he was inclined to forget, but most
important, he was a link to the past. Bushee was from
the candy store.

"Jackie had to play the mountains," recalls Bernie.
"And they all came to see him. And they all liked to
see him do the familiar things. The apartment. The
psychiatrist. His family. How he hated to pay taxes.
How he wanted to go into the army, but not during a
war. But the imitation of Ed Sullivan killed them. Had
to do it. He always did Sullivan, even before the explo-
sion. But now it was mandatory. Like a singer has to
sing certain familiar songs, he had to do his Ed Sulli-
van. Not that he is a particularly good imitator. Will
Jordan did a better imitation. But Jackie's imitation was
like an impression, a Picasso, in many ways much closer

to the spirit of Ed Sullivan. The people who came to the show wanted to see this and they would get very annoyed if they didn't get it. Tough, tough audiences."

Nevertheless, the money was always good, the food wasn't bad, and there was a semblance of safety — since he was surrounded by Jews. Come summer, the Catskills always beckoned.

And so this is how he found himself in the Las Vegas airport at 2 o'clock in the morning late in the spring of 1966. He was waiting for a connecting flight back to New York, then he would drive ninety miles up to the mountains. Suddenly, Jackie straightened up as if electricity had passed through him.

"C'mon," he said to Bushee, grabbing his arm, pulling him down the corridor. "Walk fast, I don't want to bump into that son-of-a-bitch."

Bernie looked back to see who it was that they were fleeing. It was Ed Sullivan.

They were walking fast in the opposite direction when suddenly Jackie felt an arm on his shoulder. Sullivan had caught up with him.

"Jackie! Jackie! I'm so happy to see you. Where have you been? Why haven't you been on the show lately?"

Jackie had that startled look he wears when he is facing a reality for which he is unprepared.

I was very nervous to say hello to him. Who knows how he could react. But he was so friendly, like nothing happened. I thought, Maybe it has something to do with his health. His memory had been slipping and he had had a stroke and that could affect a memory. "How are you feeling?" he asks me.

"You look good. I miss you." And then he looks at me and he says, "You want me to tell you the truth? I'm happy to see you because I always meant to tell you that I always felt terrible about what happened. I know you weren't being disrespectful and vulgar. I was just so caught up in the moment, the tension of the show, and I know I misinterpreted your gesture. All my friends told me that I made a mistake, but it's like having a fight with your wife. She proved you were wrong but somehow you're too proud to apologize and admit that you're wrong and you let the thing go on. I'd love to have you back on the show." I was so overwhelmed, I couldn't think. I said, "Why not?"

It was a stunning moment. Bushee had been at the show. He had been an eyewitness. He heard Sullivan scream at Jackie, accusing him of "giving the finger to my president." His first reaction was complete confusion. What was Sullivan screaming about? Jackie had raised a thumb at the camera, not a finger. It was a mild and funny riposte to the clumsy efforts of Sullivan to control the timing. However, so powerful was the force of Sullivan's conviction that Bushee, himself, began to doubt. He actually began to think that maybe Jackie had struck with his middle finger. It was only when he looked at films of the show that he saw clearly, plainly, and incontrovertibly that Jackie had raised not a middle finger, but a thumb at the camera.

But Sullivan had been looking at a television monitor and what he saw, the thing that stuck in his eye, was the image of the president followed by the image of

Jackie Mason raising irreverent fingers. This could only be interpreted as "giving the finger to my president" by a man of Sullivan's heightened patriotism.

Finally, in the Las Vegas Airport, Sullivan was coming around. He wanted to end the dispute, stop the lawsuit.

Back in New York, Paul O'Dwyer was against a settlement. We'll win the lawsuit, he argued. That's the only thing that the public will remember. A big fat win in the courts. To accept something less would be to leave the lingering sense of bad taste among the American public.

Jackie also admired O'Dwyers's feisty defiance. The man enjoyed a righteous battle. But Chartoff and Weber convinced him that if he did win the country would detest him and that it would be bigger to settle it on the air.

There were two factions — show biz was one faction, all pleading with me to settle. Sullivan was too powerful. Defeating Sullivan would be like rubbing the nose of the pope in dirt. He was considered holy by the American public. You'll look like a sicko and an outcast and nobody will have anything to do with you. And O'Dwyer was the other faction, begging me not to settle: "You go on the air, nobody will notice it. People don't notice people making up. They only remember the fight." But I thought it was the smart thing, to go on television and be big about it.

On Stepember 11, 1966, Ed Sullivan announced that he was bringing on an "old friend of mine and yours,

*Jackie Mason." And Jackie walked out with that slight
grin and they shook hands.*

I went on the show the next week and I did my
spot and I was never invited back again. Nobody cared
that I went on. And I had the same stigma after that
I had before. Turns out, Paul O'Dwyer was right.

A lot of people said to me after that, "Do you
think he was just trying to get out of the suit?" I
said, I don't think so. I think he was really very passionate about this whole business and he was very
sincere when he said it to me. He made a mistake. It
doesn't make sense that he wasn't sincere. Why would
he get involved in the first place if he didn't think I
did something dirty? I believe that he was sincere when
he fired me and sincere when he apologized.

*Jackie was still performing small-time club dates. ("I'm
glad you caught me on a good night. I have a feeling
some of you people out there have been caught on some
good nights. As a matter of fact, I'm willing to bet if
we turned the lights on, we could solve a couple of
bank jobs.") As always, wherever he played and whenever he played, Jackie played with fire. There was a real
sense of danger when he took the stage. Sometimes, it
went beyond the bounds of professional risk. ("Are you
people really carrying guns or are you just a tough audience?") He couldn't resist teasing the "wise guys" in
the small-time clubs. He liked to see the swaggering
wild men squirm under his professional taunts. The other
side of this coin was that he was fascinated by these
same men he half-jokingly referred to as "murderers."*

"There's a table full of murderers out front," he would tell the backstage crew and there was more than a kernel of truth neatly bottled up in that assessment.

"That's the writer talking. I knew that I could always get away with kibitzing the Italians. They were always my biggest fans from the days I started in the business. In fact, my best friend is a guy half-Italian, half-Jewish. If he can't buy it wholesale, he steals it."

Most of the mob big shots liked it when he picked on them during a show; they gave Jackie the benefit of the doubt and took the nightclub insults for show-business humor and a compliment. But the uncertain lieutenants and the trigger-happy Mafia soldiers could be very touchy about their bubble of pride and reputation.

Jackie's boyhood friend Bushee, who was there and who was Jackie's manager, remembers a close call in a nightclub on Long Island.

In Bushee's opinion, "Jackie should have been dead ten times by now. But this one time, this time he came very close to meeting his maker, this was just after the Sullivan episode. I had booked him into a small club out on Long Island. A real small shithouse.

"The thing about Jackie, he had to be working. He had no star pride that it had to be top club. He had to be in front of a crowd. Even if it was working for short money in a toilet. He didn't care just as long as he had that time on the stage. And what else did he have? He had no wife, no children. All he had was this knot in his stomach that he had to be a star. That's why he has to work.

"The Sullivan thing hurt us, even after they made up. No doubt about it. Could not get bookings and he had to take what he could get. Otherwise, he would not be working this particular spot.

"Now this club on Long Island was a mob joint. The wise guys would come in there on Friday nights with their girlfriends and on Saturday nights they would bring in their wives. You could always tell the wives because they had on a corsage. The Mafia machismo was famous for that Friday-night, Saturday-night switch.

"So, now Jackie has this thing, it's in the act, when he gets on the stage, if you're sitting up front, he's gonna pick on you. He looks down in the front row and he starts picking on people.

" 'Is that your wife, mister, because I saw you with another wife the other night. And the other wife was better looking, I'll be honest. This girl, pffft!'

"The Mafia big shots loved it. They always loved Jackie. But this one night, Jackie does the show and he picks on some guy and the guy laughs and looks comfortable, which makes Jackie go further and further in his act.

" 'Personally, I think you could do better, but if you're comfortable with this yenta, that's fine with me. She doesn't look so happy, but what does she know?'

"Jackie was heading back to the dressing room after the performance when he feels a hand grab him by the throat."

A hand! That sounds like something. This was like a steel trap. He grabs me by the throat and he says that he is gonna kill me. I am trying to talk to this

172 · *Jackie, Oy!*

man, to maybe explain, but he has me by the throat and he is not only strangling me and cutting off my air, he is preventing me from offering any kind of an explanation. Or apology. He just tells me that he is going to be waiting outside in the parking lot after the last show and he is going to kill me.

I, personally, believed him. He seemed to me to be the kind of person who was capable of murder. This occurred to me because he was murdering me by the throat at the time. So, what should I do? The man leaves me there, after leaving fingerprints up and down my throat, and he is gone. Outside, waiting to murder me. I get the owner of the club, who I happen to know is very well connected and a personal friend of many of these same type of murderers. Maybe he can help me. I explain the situation and he grasps it all very quickly. He knows about murderers and how touchy they can be when you talk about their wives. Jews, you can make fun of their wives all night and all day. But Italians place their women on a pedestal and if a comedian makes fun of them, they're liable to kill you. Period. That simple. So the owner gets on the phone and he starts to make some calls to people who are very high up in that organization and meanwhile, I have to go out and do another show. Everybody is telling me, Be careful, be careful. Don't do anything stupid because this guy could shoot you right on the stage.

Luckily, one of the calls worked. The owner comes in trailing this cement block who is all slumped and apologetic. Someone very high in one of the major crime families told him that Jackie Mason was not to be hurt.

They liked him. The guy asks sheepishly if he can introduce his girlfriend to Jackie Mason.

If they didn't shoot you on the stage, they could always get you afterward, Bushee said. In Las Vegas, when Jackie was performing at the Aladdin, there was one very muscular, tough guy in the audience, in the front row, who Jackie kept picking on throughout the whole show. "You know sex is life. If not for sex would you be here?" *Pointing at the guy, he said,* "I think you would." *He kept picking on the guy because the guy is smiling. He looks like he's having a good time. Because of the way he's smiling Jackie thinks he loves him so he picks on him all the more.* "People would never think of cheating each other in business. But if they're married they could cheat, because then they're a swinger. Don't you think that marriage should be just as holy a relationship as business? I have nothing but contempt and disgust for cheaters. Especially this one sitting right in front of me. I'm talking to you, mister! Get out!" *And later:* "You know I never cared what a person is or what he does. Here's a man — I don't care what he is or what he does. I don't care about him at all! . . . I don't like this man!" *At the end of the show, as Jackie is walking out into the casino, the tough guy comes up to him.* "I thought he wanted to shake my hand, so I said, 'Oh, you're the guy I was picking on.'" *The tough guy looked at him, scowled, and said loudly,* "Are you a Jew?" *And Jackie sized up the situation immediately and said,* "Not necessarily."

Everybody knew the mob was a fact of club life. They had silent pieces of a lot of clubs. It was a convenient method of washing their money. They also enjoyed the glamour of the business. They were, in their own way, showmen, themselves. A lot of drama went into running a mob family. Jackie made certain that he made friends with them, sat with them after the shows, talked to them, as much as he could, about the life. He flirted with danger and the mob people liked courage. They recognized something kindred about a man who took chances.

Which brought Jackie to the desert. For a full year, Jackie vanished into the desert. Not like the ten tribes. Like the lost entertainers trying to become stars. It was 1966 and he was playing the hotel lounges where there was no night and no day. He was a headline act and, as such, worth a lot of gold in Las Vegas.

He was working the Aladdin Hotel lounge with a long-term contract and he read the newspapers every day and the big story was that Frank Sinatra and Mia Farrow, after living together like hippies, finally got married. He claims that he never made any jokes about Sinatra, but even on his first album he makes teasing references to Sinatra and his unhindered life-style:

"If any ordinary fifty-year-old man marries a twenty-year-old girl, he's a dirty old man. But if his name is Frank Sinatra, he's a 'sportsman.' "

Jackie swears that he did not make such jokes. There were a lot of Jackies working Las Vegas that season: Jackie Gayle, Jackie Vernon, Jackie Canon, Jackie Leonard, Jackie Miles, Jack Carter. A few Jackie imitators. But the jokes — all of which he calls "cheap" and beneath him — were all attributed to Jackie Mason.

And so the people who got annoyed, got mad at Jackie Mason. The first call came in to his dressing room. The

*anonymous caller said, Listen, Frank don't like the joke.
Drop it.*

*Still, jokes were printed in newspaper columns, were
repeated as gossip, all ascribed to Jackie Mason.*

"I hear Sinatra is not going on a honeymoon.
They're going away to summer camp."

*The strangled voice — that peculiar Mafia dueling
scar, a mark of membership — was on the phone again.
"If you mention the name Sinatra again, we'll kill you.
Do you understand? Drop it or we'll get ya." Well,
there are a lot of nuts out there. Someone could be
trying to impress Sinatra. Someone could be making
crank phone calls. You couldn't just drop all the material because someone objected. You wouldn't have
an act.*

"Johnson makes wonderful speeches about our land.
The land is wonderful, the land is fine, the land is
good. He means his land. The rest of the country,
pfffft! They have press conferences and they ask him,
'How about unemployment?' He says, 'I didn't notice it. I'm working. As long as I'm working, everything's all right.' Goldwater. Remember Goldwater?
I didn't agree with everything he had to say, on the
other hand, he doesn't agree with everything he has
to say, either."

*Those were Jackie's jokes. He says that he never made
the joke that Frank and Mia were "going on a honeymoon — she's taking him to summer camp." But he
did make jokes about how miserable Frank Sinatra was
only he didn't know it. He did tease Sinatra about how*

psychiatrists all agree that a man who chases endless strings of young women is completely unhappy. Only Sinatra is too busy chasing women to notice how unhappy he is. He swears that this wasn't part of his current act.

It didn't stop the feud that was beginning in spite of his denials. The local press played the story over and over and, suddenly, the feud was splashed all over the big newspapers. Meanwhile, the threatening calls were endless. "We're gonna kill ya! You are dead!" The usual kind of death threats. The Aladdin security house detectives began guarding Jackie round the clock. A guard was in his room, in his dressing room, following him to meals.

And the strangled threats continued.

But a funny thing happened. The weight of public opinion began to shift to Jackie's favor. Frank Sinatra was beginning to be seen as a public bully and mean-tempered when drinking, with too much power. Newspaper columnists and photographers were punched out. He insulted women, he threw his weight around without any regard to anyone else. He was, in short, a boor.

And, if the threats were to be believed, he was worse. Jackie suspected that a lot of the rumors were true. He knew how far Sinatra's people would go to avenge "Ol' Blue Eyes' " honor. Supposedly they left people for dead after brutal beatings. But Jackie couldn't allow that to stop his career. He might be worried, but he was not afraid for his life. Not yet.

Jackie's worry was not entirely irrational. Stars had a habit of throwing their weight around. Once, before he hit big on television, Jackie had a run-in with Buddy Hackett at the Concord Hotel. According to Bernie

Weber, Hackett claimed that Jackie was stealing his material.

What material, specifically? asked Phil Greenwald, the late manager of the hotel.

Topics, said Hackett.

He's stealing topics?

He talks about the same things that I talk about.

Greenwald had been in the business long enough to know that comedians were crazy. Shecky Greene once stopped talking to Jackie Mason because Jackie sang during his act. Shecky worked at a piano and regarded comedy and music as his, exclusively. A comedian named Larry Leslie sued CBS, claiming that the six o'clock news was his idea.

But Phil Greenwald was not going to be pushed around by Buddy Hackett, admittedly a big-name star at the time. Jackie Mason was a reliable and honorable entertainer. He could always be counted on to save a sagging weekend.

If you don't get rid of Jackie Mason, I walk, threatened Hackett.

Goodbye, Greenwald told Hackett.

So, Jackie knew the danger of a wound to the pride of a show-business animal.

By the first Monday in November of 1966, it was clear that Sinatra was losing the public relations war with Jackie Mason. The hotel owners weren't firing him. The public was rooting for the little guy, Jackie Mason.

Finally, Sinatra, working down the strip at the Sands Hotel, decided to visit his old pal Joe E. Lewis, who was also on the bill with Jackie Mason. Sinatra and all his entourage came crashing into the Aladdin while

Jackie was still on stage at about one in the morning. They were very noisy.

"Do you have to bother a Jew while he is trying to make a living?" asked Jackie from the stage.

A chorus of hoots and catcalls erupted from Sinatra's table.

Sinatra was performing for his entourage. "Hey, Jackie, c'mon, let's make up, pal. Whaddaya say?"

Jackie continued. He ignored the Sinatra group.

"C'mon, you little rabbi, let's bury the hatchet."

Jackie turned and with one swift arrow, aimed at Sinatra's heart: "What's the matter, you're not busy upstairs?"

This was a reference to Sinatra's bride, Mia Farrow, who was waiting in their suite.

Bernie Weber says that Jackie left the stage and Sinatra started to hurl insults after him. "Fuck him," Sinatra called. Joe E. Lewis had come out onto the stage by now and Sinatra had his arm around the shoulder of his old crony. "We don't need him. Fuck him. The little creep."

Jackie didn't hear. His ears were burning with anger. He just kept walking.

But it was not the end of it. Sinatra glowed with rage and one unpaid debt.

CHAPTER FOURTEEN

War and Peace

On Sunday, November 6, 1966, at about six-thirty in the evening, Jackie Mason was sitting on the bed in his room in the Aladdin Hotel. There was a hotel waiter setting up a table and a bodyguard in the room. When the phone rang, Jackie got up to answer it. Just then, three .22-caliber bullets crashed through the glass door leading to the balcony and slammed into the mattress, right where Jackie had been sitting before he got up to answer the phone.

I totally, absolutely, completely absolve Frank Sinatra. He would never do such a thing. He would never approve of such a thing. It's true, he doesn't like me, he's never liked me, but he would never in this world do anything as wild as that. Maybe we don't get along, but the man is not a murderer.

Frank Sinatra had a lot of hot-blooded fans and Jackie thought that if he cooled it — if he didn't come right out and blame Sinatra, if he didn't point any fingers,

so to speak, the harassment would stop. After all, it
was only show-business schtick.

Maybe it's some kook who wants to impress Frank,
look like a big shot to him. Maybe it's a broad, but
I can't think that I hurt any broad bad enough for
this.

The Nevada police began an investigation, then
dropped it when Jackie refused to take a lie-detector
test. Despite the fact that there had been two eyewit-
nesses and there was incontrovertible proof that some-
one had clearly tried to murder Jackie Mason's mat-
tress, the authorities left the press with the unmistakable
impression that they believed that the whole thing was
a publicity stunt.

In other words, the prime suspect in the attack on
Jackie Mason was Jackie Mason.

Jackie did not go out of his way to pacify Sinatra. A
more prudent man might have sent out feelers, issued
private apologies. But since he hadn't done anything
wrong, Jackie didn't think he had any obligation to make
peace, despite the fact that there was plenty of evidence
to suggest that Sinatra was not a man who suffered in
silence blows to his wisp of dignity. The record of his
public battles makes Sean Penn seem meek.

And still, the bad jokes were made and they were
attributed to Jackie Mason, although to this day, to
this very minute, he swears he didn't say it.

"Every night, they get ready for bed. Frank soaks
his dentures and Mia soaks her braces. She takes off
her roller skates and puts them next to his cane. He
peels off his toupee and she unbraids her hair."

Jackie thought that Sinatra's "people" should know that he makes better jokes than that. But now it was getting out of hand. The feud even broke out of the confines of the Nevada desert. One week after the gunshots, Phil Greenwald was talking to police in upstate New York. He was telling them that he'd been threatened with death if he booked Jackie Mason at the Concord Hotel. The detectives listened with that bored, half-lidded skepticism cops love to display when they suspect that they are being used in some sordid media ploy.

Just then, as the detectives were interviewing him, Greenwald got another one of those calls. The voice, belonging to a very angry woman, said Greenwald would be shot dead if he booked Jackie Mason into the hotel. The detectives were listening in on an extension. They began to take seriously the threats on Jackie Mason and his friends. But what were they to do? They could guard Phil Greenwald, but Jackie Mason was half a continent away, under the authority of a completely indifferent jurisdiction.

Meanwhile, there were still the inflammatory jokes by this troublemaker impersonator making the rounds, again, attributed to Jackie Mason.

"I see Sinatra'a got another girl. Boy, the way he goes from one girl to another, any psychiatrist will tell you that that denotes a basic insecurity. I should be so insecure. Doesn't bother the girls that he has elevators on his shoes and his hair is a gift from an admirer."

On November 21, two weeks after the telephoned threats to Greenwald, Jackie had finished the last show at the Aladdin. It was four in the morning and a woman friend drove him to the airport. A few weeks before, Jackie borrowed a hundred dollars in cash from an airport employee and now he was paying it back. He didn't know that someone else was out to pay him back at the same time.

Jackie repaid the money and hung around the airport, then headed back to the hotel. His friend was at the wheel of the car. It was, by now, 6:40 in the morning. They were driving along Paradise Road when Jackie saw a car coming at them, head-on. This is what he told the press afterward:

"It was a Plymouth. I can still see it. It starts to come across the double line and smacks into us. She's all right, although my face and head are cut and my knees are pretty badly banged up. I went right into the rearview mirror. I get out and go to see who this person is and I can see that she was drinking. She told me, 'I wasn't driving. It's not my fault. The man was driving.' I looked around and I didn't see any man. She was the driver.

"Then we heard the Highway Patrol coming and she opened the door and ran down the gully, heading toward the desert."

He was interviewed at Southern Nevada Memorial Hospital where he was treated for his injuries.

Jackie decided maybe it was time to get out of Las Vegas. He headed for Miami, where he worked the winter season. He was booked into the Saxony when he was approached by two men in the lobby. "Listen, we don't like what you said about Frank." "Wise guys," the connected mob killers, all had that sly wink. Jackie should publicly state that Sinatra was innocent, they seemed to suggest, maybe even did suggest out loud. You don't want to start a blood feud with a crazy Sicilian who could conceivably put a hurt on you. This is what the mob guys suggested with that raised eyebrow.

I did not believe that Sinatra was behind this. To this day, I do not believe that he had anything to do with it. But there are plenty of crazy people out there who want to do him a favor and if they hear that he doesn't get along with a certain comedian, they could believe that scaring him will be a favor.

I'll tell you the truth, you don't know what's out there. You stand up on a stage and you look out into an audience and you have no idea what kind of sick maniacs could be waiting to attack you after the show. No matter what you say. You can't let this rule your life. You can't be controlled by crazy people who think that they are going to make a name for themselves by attacking a celebrity.

Just Jackie's luck, at the start of 1967, Frank Sinatra and his entourage took over Miami Beach; they were filming Tony Rome. *In the nightclub of the Saxony Hotel, one of those second-ranked hotels where the audience was just a little noisy, where the hecklers felt unrestrained because of the peeling paint and shabby rugs, Jackie Mason made one small, meaningless joke. Not even a joke. A reference. Hardly anything worth mentioning. But someone among the crowd was listening.*

"I don't know who took a shot at me but afterward I heard somebody singing doobie, doobie do."

Two men approached Jackie Mason as he was walking along Collins Avenue in downtown Miami Beach. They were not the kind of men who would be looking for an autograph and they bore the hash marks of their trade: thick necks, thick arms, tree-stump bodies, and cold, dead fish eyes. "You don't take a hint, do you?" said one. The other just hung back like a block of wood, poised to smash. "You were told to lay off mentioning Mr. Sinatra. We are going to have to get drastic if you don't shut that big mouth."

Jackie didn't report the threat. What was the point? Everyone thought that he was a publicity hound. There were at least three other threats. One even took place in the lobby of the hotel. But nothing stopped the jokes ascribed to the innocent Jackie Mason.

"I found out. They're not really married. She's just another bodyguard. Frank has to stay up night and day, day and night, guarding her body."

At 5:30 in the morning of February 13, 1967, after his last show at the Saxony and after coffee at the Rascal House, Jackie was sitting in his car in front of his apartment building, talking to a receptionist. Suddenly, the door of the car flew open, a voice said, "We warned you about using Sinatra material in your act," and a huge, hard, ham fist flew in Jackie's face. Jackie claims he didn't hear it, he was too busy getting beaten up, but the receptionist remembered.

There were seven or eight blows. Jackie's nose was broken, several bones in his cheek were crushed, and there were a lot of bruises and contusions. "This time they really got me," he told a reporter from the New York Post from Jackson Memorial Hospital where he was being treated. "My whole face is busted up. It was obviously a professional job. The guy didn't say a word and he threw the punches fast, like a professional fighter."

He said that he tried to chase the guy in his car, but this is probably just post-beating bravado. What would he have done if he had caught up with him?

I would have given him a good piece of my mind. Who does he think he is, hitting a star? Well, maybe not a star, but almost. I was just waiting. Every Jew comes one word away from killing someone. You hear it all the time: "If he said one more word." What that word is, no one knows. If they ever find out, murder. That guy was lucky I couldn't figure out what the hell that word was. I had to get to the hospital before I bled to death.

At the end of March, Jackie returned to Las Vegas. He had been shot at, run down, threatened, beaten up. His brothers had warned him to lay off the Sinatra jokes. He said, I'm innocent. Even if you're innocent, lay off. Don't even make jokes. Not that anyone believed he was innocent. He could be innocent, but it was not believed.

All the attacks and all the threats had taken a toll. He thought: "I could be killed!" Then he thought, "It

*would definitely be a front-page story!" Then he thought,
"Boy, is that a sick need for attention!" Still, prudence
marked the rest of that year.*

It was old news. The columns stopped mentioning
it. I never mentioned it. I'll tell you the truth, I thought
it would be in bad taste from the beginning. Not
funny. If something is funny, I don't care if they send
a Nazi panzer division after me, I'll use it. Because
I'll tell you something: I'm more afraid of not being
funny than I'm afraid of a Nazi panzer division.

CHAPTER FIFTEEN

Too Jewish

Frank Sinatra's army wasn't the only war that Jackie Mason fought that year. There was also the incident between Israel and Egypt and Jordan and Syria. It was called the Six-Day War. He got mixed up in that dispute, too.

"Jackie was going to break the Egyptian blockade," recalls Bushee.

Weeks before the opening of hostilities, the Egyptians threw the United Nations' observers out of the Sinai Desert, closed the Gulf of Aqaba to Israeli shipping, sealing off the port city of Elath (a casus belli since the gulf was protected by international agreement and was imperative to the Israeli economy), and began making warlike threats.

A feeling of helplessness engulfed a lot of American Jews who did not fully appreciate the high quality of the Israeli army. Against so many armies and so much Russian technology, Israel, they feared, was doomed.

That whole spring was not unlike that summer of 1940, the false peace, when the world waited for the German army to slash through France.

Like a lot of American Jews, Jackie Mason believed that someone had to do something! He was, after all, a Jew. And a Jew of a particular generation. It was his generation that suffered and witnessed the Holocaust. Israel represented, if not vindication for that impossible sacrifice, at least some small consolation, some redeeming nugget of hope. As a child, he had helped contribute to the blue-and-white collection boxes spread around in Jewish communities to buy land in Palestine for a Jewish national homeland.

It was not a biblical commitment. The secular Jews believed in a homeland as a practical necessity because they knew that in the end, no one else would come to save a Jew. There stirred in every Jewish heart a flutter of pride when the fragment became a nation. And that pride almost exploded out of every Jewish chest when — despite all forecasts that they would be hurled into the sea — the tiny nation defeated five Arab armies. Nineteen years later, it still seemed such a fragile thing. The Israelis lived under the unsheathed sword of sworn enemies. It was a time when they seemed vulnerable.

Jackie could not sit idly by making jokes while Israel went into the toilet (as show-business people would irreverently put it).

Not long before, there had been an Israeli civilian, Abie Nathan, who owned a restaurant in Tel Aviv and was also a pilot. He had flown a plane to Egypt, trying to make peace all by himself. The gesture was romantic and dramatic and a little silly — in other words, it had all the ingredients that would appeal to a man like Jackie

Mason. The fact that it didn't work was only a small detail. But Jackie couldn't duplicate Abie Nathan's flight to Cairo. First of all, they'd shoot him down because the Egyptians had, by now, improved their air defenses. Second, Jackie was not too crazy about flying in flimsy airplanes.

So, he sent Bushee to Atlanta to buy a boat.

"What kind of a boat?" asked Bushee.

"A big boat," replied Jackie.

"What are we going to do with this big boat?"

"We are going to paint the name 'Peace' on the side and then we are going to sail across the Atlantic, through the Mediterranean and break the Egyptian blockade," said Jackie.

Bushee was used to Jackie's imaginative flights of fancy, but this seemed to have a certain ring of wild absurdity, not to mention terrible danger.

"You know how to sail a big ship?" Bushee asked.

"Putz, we'll get a crew," said Jackie, who had already worked out the logistical aspects of this adventure.

"What about the Palace?"

"What about it? If they invite us, we'll go. Otherwise, fuck 'em."

"No. No. Caesars Palace. In Las Vegas. You're supposed to appear. You're getting twelve and a half thousand dollars a week, it's the most you've ever made."

"Are you kidding me? Jews are dying over there. Do you actually think my own personal fate means anything whatsoever compared to that? Do you believe that I'm that despicable a character that I would for a second consider the consequences to my own career when the fate of my people hangs in the balance by a slim

*thread? Are you such a lowlife that you could actually
believe —*"

"*Jackie, we have a contract.*"

"*Oh, a contract. Well, that's different. I'll talk to the
owners; it'll be all right. Go. Get a boat.*"

*Bernie Weber went down to Atlanta and found an
old Liberty ship from World War II. With a lot of work
and some luck, it might make one more passage across
the Atlantic. The plan was to load it with medical sup-
plies and run it through the Egyptian blockade. "We'll
put red crosses and peace signs all over it, don't worry,"
assured Jackie.*

*Bushee put a four-hundred-dollar bond down to buy
the ship and was going through all the details of the
transaction through shipping experts when, on June 6,
the shooting war actually broke out. Israel staged a
preemptive strike against Egypt.*

*Bushee called Jackie in Las Vegas and broke the news.
Jackie was shocked, but he was on a plane heading east
before nightfall.*

"*Get us there,*" *said Jackie.* "*I don't care how you
arrange it, but get us into Israel.*"

*It was easier said than done. Israel was in a state of
war and had cut itself off from the rest of the world.
They wanted no hint of what was going on at the battlefronts to leak out. Already, although no one knew
it, the war was won. Israel had destroyed the Egyptian
air force on the ground in the first few hours, driven
their armies out of the Sinai, and were already turning
their armored spearheads toward the Golan Heights.*

*But to ensure their freedom of action, they allowed
the Arab radio to claim phony victories. The only*

thing that the world knew was the Arab claims of con-
quest and the ominous Israeli silence. Which played
into Israel's strategic hands but made a lot of Jews
nervous.

Volunteers who wanted to fight were clamoring to
get into Israel; they were turned away from Israeli con-
sulates and embassies around the world. There were a
few special flights to bring in the doctors who had been
secretly recruited, but even military reservists had trou-
ble getting back to their units.

"I had some friends in Bobby Kennedy's office," re-
calls Bushee, who had worked as a volunteer on his
1966 Senate campaign. "Jackie didn't actually work for
him, but he spoke up for him, he supported him, and
they knew this. I pulled whatever string I could pull in
the Kennedy office. So we got a plane. It wasn't El Al,
all the El Al pilots were back in the service. The only
thing we could get was Olympia, the Greek airline, and
even that was very tough. We were the only Americans
on the flight. It went to Athens and it was supposed to
go on to Tel Aviv.

"On the plane, Jackie talked about the war. He
worked on some jokes. Couldn't use Borscht Belt ma-
terial in Israel. He knew that. He always knew what
was appropriate. He's like an animal on the stage. He
can hear a twig break."

See, at the time, you had Bob Hope doing shows
in Vietnam. I used to think, You wanna stop the wars,
kill Bob Hope. America can't hold a war without
Bob Hope. And I also thought, somewhere in the back
of my mind, I'll be the Bob Hope of Israel. I'll put
on a show and I'll be just like Bob Hope.

The brand-new Olympia Airline 747 landed in Athens and there it stayed. The flight to Lod Airport outside Tel Aviv was delayed indefinitely.

And so Jackie and Bushee walked around Athens. "Where are the broads?" asked Jackie, who was now regarding himself as the heroic soldier in need of comfort on his last night before battle. He wasn't interested in the Parthenon or the Acropolis. He wanted "broads."

They found — what else? — a coffee shop. They sat in a Greek coffee shop in downtown Athens and admired the Greek women.

"They come out in the evening and they travel in groups," recalls Bushee.

Look at this, just like the Hasidim. Chaperones and everything. They walk around in the afternoon and they stroll by the men sitting in the sidewalk cafés sipping coffee. Women want to be seen and men want to see. It's the same the world over. Under a blue sky. Not far away, that same sky was filled with killer jets.

That night, Olympia resumed its flight to Tel Aviv and Jackie and Bushee landed at Lod Airport. They taxied up to the loading gate and when they looked out the window, Jackie could see the sign over the tower announcing the name of the airport. In Hebrew.

No one can explain this. You hear about it. People tell you what it feels like to land in a Jewish country — a whole country of Jews! But there is no way to explain the feeling. You fly into an airport and you look up and you see on the buildings Hebrew letters. Hebrew! Letters that I learned as a boy on the Lower East Side in Hebrew School. Here they are on official buildings, on military aircraft. Not something you have to hide from the *goyim* so they won't beat you up on the way home from school. Not something that you have to be ashamed of. Official Hebrew letters! Nothing prepares you for that. We sat there in the airplane, the two of us, looking out the window as we taxied up to the ramp, and our hearts were in our throats. We couldn't speak. We could hardly breathe.

They were given a room in the Tel Aviv Hilton. The hotel had been commandeered by the military. Only the press and soldiers lived there. Jackie and Bushee walked through the lobby and into the bar. There were the familiar faces of the American evening news programs, the anchormen. A lot of them were trying to live up to the great myth of war correspondents and were falling down drunk.

Jackie and Bushee walked out into the Tel Aviv night. There was still a blackout, but the city had a life and vibrancy that was exciting. Mandy Rice Davies had a club. Everyone seemed to have a club in Tel Aviv. There might have been a war on, but there was no gloom on Dizengov Street.

Jackie had a bright idea. He sent Bushee out to hire a camera crew. He wanted to film his trip to the battlefronts. Maybe he would make a Bob Hope–type special out of it.

But all the cameramen were called up into the army. Finally, Bushee found a few cameramen and they filmed a lot of the trip. Afterward, when the trip was over, the cameramen said that the film was spoiled. They claimed that it had inadvertently been ruined. "I thought, 'Yeah, maybe,'" said Bushee. "I thought maybe, also, this was a good way for the Israelis to unofficially stop us — get some lame cameramen and ruin the film. This was smarter than looking uncooperative."

They didn't know who I was and Bernie Weber was running around to the generals and admirals telling them that Jackie Mason is here. They said, "We have a war to run. Who cares if Jackie Mason is here? Nobody here is looking for Jackie Mason. We're looking for the enemy." And he is arguing and hocking, "But he could do so much for the people, for the morale," and they said, "The only thing he can do is to fight. If he can't fight, he can't serve any purpose." He says, "Yeah, but he'll tell them jokes." They said, "There's nothing to laugh at, there's a war going on. People are getting killed and we don't need comedians now."

But I was not gonna be stopped. They were barricading the hotel because they were afraid of bombs and we went out into the street. Carefully, but we went out. There's a war, but we went sightseeing. Here are the streets where the Jewish nation came back to life. Here are the places I have read about. The homeland. It was very moving. Not that anything was open. This was closed. That was closed. Everybody went to the war. But there were some clubs and some entertainment and it wasn't a complete waste of time. Finally, we got back to the hotel and there's a colonel or something waiting for us. A girl.

Dr. Ruth Westheimer picks up a few points from Jackie about you-know-what.

Carol Channing's best friends are sometimes diamonds in the rough.

Pat Kennedy Lawford did not understand one single joke.

Jackie distracts Angela Lansbury as he attempts to steal her watch.

Lauren Bacall reacts to the suggestion that Jackie is a lot like Bogie.

Kirk Douglas was so impressed by the show that he said next time he came he would wear a necktie.

Tom Hanks and Kathleen Turner, male and female finalists in the Jackie Mason look-alike contest.

Nick Vanoff, producer of the Broadway show, and Jon Peters, producer of *Caddyshack II*, flank Jackie at Sardi's.

Jyll Rosenfeld, who, some say, engineered Jackie's comeback, accepts the blame.

Jackie pondering the world, which now belongs to him.

Dr. Ruth Westheimer picks up a few points from Jackie about you-know-what.

Carol Channing's best friends are sometimes diamonds in the rough.

Pat Kennedy Lawford did not understand one single joke.

JUDIE BERSTEIN

Jackie distracts Angela Lansbury as he attempts to steal her watch.

Lauren Bacall reacts to the suggestion that Jackie is a lot like Bogie.

Kirk Douglas was so impressed by the show that he said next time he came he would wear a necktie.

Tom Hanks and Kathleen Turner, male and female finalists in the Jackie Mason look-alike contest.

Nick Vanoff, producer of the Broadway show, and Jon Peters, producer of *Caddyshack II*, flank Jackie at Sardi's.

Jyll Rosenfeld, who, some say, engineered Jackie's comeback, accepts the blame.

Jackie pondering the world, which now belongs to him.

Very pretty. Some army they got there! They figured,
"Well, the war is almost won, if this guy wants to
work for nothing, we'll take him."

*They were in a jeep on the road to Hebron, right
behind the Israeli paratroopers. They could see smoke
in the distance, but the thing that struck them, the thing
that they couldn't get over, was the tanks lying on the
side of the road. So quiet. They were almost undam-
aged. Lying on their sides. Like they were sleeping. If
you looked close you could see one shot, one wound.
That was all it took. The Israelis had advanced homing
devices even then.*

*At first, there was only the first thrill of pride, that
Israelis were so technically efficient, that they were not
the pale, thin yeshiva boys who could not stand up in
a fair fight. These boys could fight!*

*But then, lying beside the sleeping tanks were these
little piles of ashes. Jackie looked closer and he realized
that he was looking at a dead human being. Not clean.
Not efficient. Deadly. It was war.*

So I had to have a routine and I started with this
one shot business. "No wasted ammunition. You
know why? This is the only country that runs a budget war. Israel makes a soldier pay for the ammunition! That's why everybody's such a good shot." Then,
I said, "You know why they only went two hundred
miles, instead of invading Egypt? Because the tanks
were rented. Hertz rent-a-tank. After two hundred
miles, there's a mileage charge. If they tried Avis instead of Hertz, and got unlimited mileage, by now
they'd be in Moscow."

The next day, a colonel came by the hotel and said, "Okay, if you still want to entertain the troops, we have just liberated Jerusalem. If you wanna go, go."

He didn't hesitate. They put him in a jeep and Jackie was working on the routine, moving toward the front, when a truck just ahead of the jeep hit a mine. The truck lifted off the ground and fell and started burning. There were wounded soldiers scattered over the rocky landscape on the road to Hebron. He could hear the screams and see the blood.

I thought, "They're all dead." You could see the blood pouring out. They couldn't last long. Then, like a miracle, a helicopter came down. Not in minutes. Seconds. And out came the doctors. Not medics. Doctors. Surgeons. Working on these soldiers before I even knew what happened. Lifting them out of there, with the smoke and the fire, like nothing I'd ever seen before. Like nothing I could ever believe.

And then a colonel comes over to the jeep and says, "Listen, if this is too much for you we can take you out of here. We can fly you back to Tel Aviv. Because this area is not entirely safe. There are still mines and there could be snipers." No, I said. We came to do something. Let's go. My heart was in my throat, but I didn't want to show fear. Not after what these boys had been going through.

But I could see that what I was doing was a very small thing compared to what was going on around me. Here was death and sacrifice — some very serious business.

They put on the show in the captured barracks of the Trans Jordan troops in Nabulus. It was the only

*air-conditioned barracks in the entire Middle East. They
had a singer, Geula Gil, an actor, and then the American comedy star Jackie Mason.*

*The exhausted soldiers stood holding their automatic
weapons, their faces smeared with the smoke and grime
of battle, their eyes still looking at death. There were a
few hundred — not like the massive shows that Bob
Hope put on. But they were paratroopers. The elite.
The soldiers who took back the Wailing Wall. What
would his father think now? What would he say if he
could see Jackie standing there on that sacred soil,
bringing comfort to the soldiers of Zion?*

I stunk the house down. They didn't know who I
was. I thought this would be some kind of USO-type
show, but they didn't know what the hell I was talking about. Big, big soldiers with red berets, they had
just destroyed seven armies and liberated Jerusalem
and they looked at me like I was the enemy. Like
they wanted to wipe me out. I think they forgot about
the Arabs. I think they would have been happier to
get me than the Arabs. At least the Arabs weren't
torturing them. Maybe they thought they were taken
prisoner and this was the torture.

*"He really saved the day," recalls Bushee. "They didn't
speak English well. Maybe broken English. And they
certainly couldn't pick up the quick New Yorkese. They
couldn't keep up with Jackie's pacing and timing. So,
he sees that the psychiatrist routine and the apartment
routine and even the material he wrote on the plane is
going nowhere, he's dying here, and he goes over to
one of these paratroopers, guy who's maybe six-foot-
seven, and there's Jackie more than a foot shorter, and*

*he says, 'How would you like a punch in the nose?'
That broke them up. That, they thought was funny. So
he started to abuse them, up and down the line, and he
became a hit."*

*He did one show. He went around and talked to some
soldiers. "How come you're not in school instead of
wasting your time playing with guns?" He drove to the
Golan Heights and looked across the mountain at Syria.
"Does your mother know that you kill people?" He
heard artillery in the distance, but he didn't bother to
put on another show. He was not Bob Hope and these
were not American troops.*

*"Frankly," he whispered to Bushee one night after a
long day of shows, "they don't look Jewish."*

*They were big and blond and had that look of fight-
ers. Some of them wore yarmulkes and there were a
disproportionate number of soldiers who wore glasses.
But Jackie did not feel at home in Israel. They were
brave and they kept alive a flame that was necessary,
but they were not really his people.*

It proved to me my ignorance about the Israelis in
terms of the culture and the language barrier that I
didn't know existed to that extent.

*And when they were on the plane coming home, Jackie
turned to Bushee and said, "Too Jewish." And Bushee
smiled and nodded.*

CHAPTER SIXTEEN

El Yid

The hard, scuffling years — the late '60s through the mid-80s — were for Jackie Mason a frenzy of activity. He turned this way and that, searching for some escape from his nightmare obscurity. He thought he might do a cable talk show. Or a TV pilot. Or a movie. Or a play. He schemed and plotted to get off the sour tread-mill between Miami and Las Vegas and the Catskill Mountains. He worked the tables, introducing himself, ingratiating himself, at the Sands in Atlantic City and, more than once, was treated like an unclean hand trying to wipe a car windshield.

"How do you do, how do you do, my name is Jackie Mason. . . ."

"We're in the middle of dinner."

The rebuke was like a window shut in his face.

Listen, I didn't live bad. I had money to buy clothes. I had enough to eat. I flew first class. I had to fly first class to keep up appearances. Not that I could afford it. Now that I can afford to fly first class I buy my ticket and wait until the plane takes off and go back into coach so I can sleep across four seats. And maybe I had to wait for a sale to buy a suit (it's a sin to buy retail anyway) and maybe it's also true that I had some disappointment, but to paint it as a grim and miserable life, like Charles Dickens!? This isn't true. I made a lot of money, but I also spent a lot of money trying to become a star. It's not like I was suffering, suffering, suffering in some dark, dirty miserable place. I was suffering a little. I was mostly comfortable.

When the wisps of opportunity — the talk-show pilots that he couldn't sell; the would-be sit-coms that never got farther than a lunch date with a network underling; the movies pasted together with future earnings that never got released; the concerts that went half sold; the plays that opened and closed like a yawn — floated out of reach, he fired managers and nagged agents and questioned civilians everywhere about what they would like to see, what he should do with himself. He was a possessed market researcher with this fabulous product — himself — and only lacking the right marketing strategy.

And, always, there was the humiliating sting of Rodney Dangerfield. Once, Dangerfield trailed Jackie around the mountains like a moonstruck groupie. He worshipped and studied at Jackie's feet, wrote him jokes, praised his gifts. Now Dangerfield began to perform and, miracle of miracles, became a large success. His "I-don't-get-no-respect" routine struck some reflexive chord in the public. They, too, felt unappreciated. They, too, felt a want of esteem. Dangerfield's incompetence,

*his bug-eyed nervous energy, his deep cynicism found
a home among America's cultural orphans.*

He started to become a bigger and bigger star and
my career was stuck where it was. Then he opened
his club, Dangerfield's, on First Avenue and I used to
work for him. Every six weeks or so, I'd appear for
a week in his club and I used to bump into him because he owned the club and he'd tell me how he
was doing — on this show, on that show, doing Carson, doing Merv. Very busy. And he'd say, "What
are you doing?" He knew what I was doing. I was
working for him. He employed me. His booking agent
got me through the Rapp agency which still handles
me, so he knew what I was doing.

As soon as I opened my mouth to say I might be
doing something else, he would turn white or change
the subject. He was in a panic to think that I might
be doing something of any value. Carl Reiner and
Steve Martin were always fans of mine and when a
nice part opened up in a movie they were making
called *The Jerk,* they offered it to me. This made
Dangerfield crazy. He was doing much better than
me. The man was making twenty-five thousand dollars for a one-nighter and I was getting five, six thousand. It came back to me from some of my friends
that he couldn't stand the thought that I got a part
in a picture. His manager tells my manager, "Why
did Jackie have to tell him about *The Jerk?* I can't
live with this man anymore."

The reason he accepted the part in *Caddyshack* was
because I was in *The Jerk.* It killed him that I got a

part in a major motion picture — a Steve Martin vehicle. But Dangerfield couldn't stand it that I got a picture. There was nobody as ambitious as him because when he had to do a Johnny Carson show, he would not just know what he was going to do, he would know it to the second.

I thought that I was an exacting, intense person until I met him. He made me look like I was on vacation. He studied every routine down to the second, he practiced every word, every gesture, marched up and down, trying out the jokes. He won't take a Carson show more than every six weeks because it takes him that long to make every word perfect. It had to be timed exactly, word for word, that he was going to do six minutes on the spot, three minutes on the couch. That's why every time he was on the Carson show, he'd never let Carson interrupt him and Carson knew he shouldn't. Carson would just say, "Hello," and Rodney went on with his jokes, one after the other. Somebody would say something, like, "This weather is killing me," and it would mix him up completely, because he would have it programmed like a symphony to the precise second.

It's hard to say why I became such an intense outlet for his jealousy and his venom. I'm playing in his club, making six, seven thousand dollars a week. He's making a hundred thousand dollars a week playing Vegas. But he enjoyed the feeling of watching me toil like a prisoner in that club. To come back from a tour and movie and tell me how great he's doing while I'm working his room, making him even more money by being his prisoner. It's like I'm operating a prison and I'm booking you in my prison while I'm running General Motors.

By 1969, Jackie was beginning to suspect that he was not going to be struck by that same bolt of lightning that made him a star in the first place. He would have to manufacture his own electricity. Bushee was having troubles at home and had moved into Jackie's new two-bedroom apartment on 56th Street (like all the others, motel-modern with no discernible hand in the decor) and together, they began working on a play.

There's a very funny process, this success. You have to be in something that catches on. A movie. Another way is a national commercial. If you're particularly colorful in that commercial, an hour later you become a sensation, like Dangerfield did with the Miller Lite Beer commercials. Dangerfield told me that the thing most responsible for the degree of his stardom was the commercials. *Caddyshack* came along and that helped, but his initial stardom did not come from the movies or from Johnny Carson, even though he did that twenty times, he was still not a major star from Johnny Carson. But the commercials made him.

Another way to become a national star is a Broadway show. If the Broadway show succeeds. If I could get a Neil Simon type of comedy, I could be a star. But Neil Simon didn't want me in 1969, so I decided to write my own play. It was a complete comedy and it took me six months to write it and I raised my own money. In those days, it cost about two hundred thousand dollars to put on a play. Not all the money came from me, about half came from Louis Wolfson, the big millionaire who was an investor and eventually went to jail for manipulating money on Wall Street.

The play was called A Teaspoon Every Four Hours, *and the plot was simple. Maybe too simple. A Jewish man (Jackie) has a son who gets involved with a Gentile. She is also black. Jackie, a cab driver in the play, goes to meet the mother of the girl, to get her assistance in breaking up the misalliance, and sure enough, they fall in love. The son and the father marry the daughter and the mother. A naïve solution to the racial strife of that season.*

While he was hard at work on the play, he was booked for a guest appearance on "The Smothers Brothers Comedy Hour." He taped the material and the CBS censor went to work with a scissor.

I needed some material for the Smothers Brothers' show and I was looking in the newspaper and I saw that we are worried about Cuba. Another item in the paper was that they're having delays at Kennedy Airport. I also read that five people were mugged in Central Park. So, I made a routine out of it during the taping. "They don't have to worry about Cuba. First of all, how are they gonna land? It takes an hour to circle and two hours to get through customs and by then they'll be worn out. You ever see people coming in from a trip? Second, even if they do land, how are they gonna get past Central Park? You think we don't have guerrillas? The whole Cuban army will get mugged." Well, somebody got offended and they cut ninety seconds out of the routine. Very substantial. So, I decided to sue. Was it a real suit? Did I have serious intentions of winning the case in a court? That truth is, I was looking more for publicity than I was out to defend the First Amendment. It wasn't a serious suit and it wasn't treated as a serious lawsuit, although it got a lot of serious publicity. It was a very serious publicity suit.

In March of 1969, Jackie filed a twenty-million-dollar suit against CBS for censoring his act. Not only that, he demanded that he be allowed to testify before the United States Senate on how he had been denied his First Amendment rights. He wanted to appear before the Senate subcommittee on communications.

By now, Bobby Chartoff was pulling away from Jackie's career. With Jackie's financial help, he went out to Hollywood and started producing films. They swore that they would remain close, but it wasn't possible, not a continent apart. All of Jackie's friends were falling away. The relationship between Jackie and Bernie Weber was growing brittle, even as Bernie was helping write the play with Mike Mortman and living in Jackie's apartment.

Jackie's sister-in-law Edythe, the wife of his brother Gabe, was handling the day-to-day business operations, paying the bills, keeping track of the club dates, fielding the offers, arranging Jackie's transportation and hotels. Gabe came to the shows, Jackie came to Friday-night dinner. There was a bond between the brothers that the wives were not permitted to share.

The play, meanwhile, took shape, and it was received for what it was: a slight, sentimental version of racial idealism.

The first preview at the ANTA Theater was in the spring of 1969, just about the time he started fighting with CBS. Ninety-seven previews later, the play opened. It was June 15, 1969, and the first mystery was the title, A Teaspoon Every Four Hours. *Why it had such a name was lost in the rewrites and historic number of previews. At some point, presumably,* A Teaspoon Every Four Hours *made sense to someone. By opening night, nothing seemed to make sense to the critics.*

How could it? The play changed every day. Because after every preview, Jackie came out front and took questions from the audience. He held a seminar. How did you like the play? What worked? What didn't work? How was this character?

It was Jackie playing market researcher again and what he couldn't seem to get through his head was that people who are stuck for an opinion, or who have vague or unformed or stupid opinions, are still going to try to sound as if they have a definite idea of how to fix this play and make it perfect.

Every night, they said, Change this line, put that piece of furniture there, walk here, then — perfect!

And every night, Jackie listened to them until he had the confusion of ninety-seven opinions and he couldn't even remember where he put the title.

Clive Barnes's review the next day in the New York Times seemed to capture the negative, dismissive attitude of the critics:

"I realized it was not a particularly distinguished play when at the intermission, I found myself rush-

ing up the aisle for a cigarette outside. It was not until I got out there that I remembered that I don't smoke."

The simple fact about Broadway is that 99 percent of the time, if the critics louse up a play and say it stinks, nobody shows up. It dies immediately. They felt it was presumptuous of me — a guttural character who has no business on Broadway — and when I opened they couldn't wait to say, "This is not a show that belongs on Broadway." The play, itself, was great. Audiences laughed. Critics didn't laugh. But audiences loved it. I had to wait sometimes twelve minutes for them to stop laughing.

The backer, Louis Wolfson, didn't want to open. He didn't think the play was ready. He had put up two hundred thousand dollars and he was beginning to think it was a bad investment. But, as usual, Jackie was impatient and impetuous. He assumed the responsibility and the debt and he opened the play on Saturday night. And when the flood of bad notices came in, he posted a closing notice.

A Teaspoon Every Four Hours *had ninety-seven previews and one performance.*

There was a flurry of club dates in the mountains and across the country to meet the debt. At the same time, Jackie changed apartments, as if he could no longer bear any of the material details of his life. He moved to 57th Street, one block away. He never stayed long in an apartment. He was a nomad who left no tracks. Someone else — a manager, an agent, a friend — picked his ties, attended to his laundry. If he needed a chair, someone else picked it out. All Jackie cared about was that something be there when he sat down.

If he suffered a setback on Broadway, maybe he could make it up on the goal line. On April 16, 1970, he got a group of show-business investors together to try to buy the New York Jets. He had TV-radio personality Joe Franklin, restaurateur Abe Margolies, and his Wall Street lawyer and crony, Leon Charney, offer sixteen million dollars for the team. "I would love to see every game for nothing," Jackie quipped. "To me that's very important."

But was it a serious offer? Did he have any money?

I was talking through my hat. What did I know about football? I didn't have two dimes to rub together. I was still paying off the show. But, it got a lot of interest, it kept my name before the public, and it made me realize that I don't like football that much.

The break with Bobby Chartoff was long and painful. Chartoff went off to Hollywood and produced a movie. Then he produced Point Blank *with Lee Marvin. There was no moment when he stopped taking Jackie's calls, he was just busier and busier, in meetings and on sets, and the calls became more and more pointless.*

I can't remember when it happened, exactly, to the second, but after a year or two of him being a producer, I saw that he wasn't going to go out of his way to help me. Before he left for Hollywood, he said to me, "You gave me money far past what I was due, and you helped me become a producer, and as soon as I become a producer, my greatest ambition in life is to be able to help you and I'll do anything in the world for you if I can catch on as a producer."

I didn't bother him after the first picture, which was an Elvis Presley picture. I didn't bother him after the second picture, the Lee Marvin picture. Then he made a third picture, *Up the Sandbox,* I believe it was, and I called him up long distance a couple of times to say, "Why don't you put me in a picture?"

I'd like to, he says, I'm trying to, it's not easy because people say you're too Jewish and that's not easy to break through, don't think it's easy, but I'm gonna get past them.

I brought it up a couple more times and he would feel nervous and self-conscious and I could see basically he didn't want to hear it, didn't want to talk to me. Finally, I asked if he'll ever find me a picture? I said, "Do you think it's fair that a guy who did so much for you in your whole life, that he gave you every penny he's got to do whatever you pleased and helped you build up your business and made you what you are, the least you could do is get me an audition if you can't get me a job. You're the producer of ten pictures already. You think I don't know how much power you have? You could do something."

And again it's: I swear to you I can't. I would like to, it's not easy, where you gonna be Thursday, I'll see you Monday . . . He was always trying to avoid me.

The end was almost chilling. Once, they spoke five times a day, even when they were across the country from each other. Once, they both put their heads together and spoke about Jackie's career, Jackie's interests, Jackie's humor. Now, Chartoff was a big shot, a major producer, among the Hollywood aristocracy, appreciated by the graduates of Princeton and Brown, all of whom thought Jackie Mason was a vulgar Catskill comic.

Somehow, Jackie got the impression that the opinion was beginning to be shared by his former manager and friend. He would never utter such a thing, but he made a living among people who believed it. He ate with them. He socialized with them. He managed to get no work for Jackie.

Finally, Jackie wrote Chartoff a long, complaining letter trying to appeal to his conscience and reminding him of all his contributions to the success of Chartoff's career.

Let's be honest. I'm the guy who was personally responsible for Chartoff. I encouraged him to go to Hollywood to try to become a producer. In fact, for the first two, three years that Chartoff and Winkler were in business, I still sent them commissions from all my income so they could stay in business. Okay, of course I had selfish motives. The first was my desperate need to be a movie star. And secondarily, Chartoff really was not good as a manager. But because I liked him and felt so close to him, I never had the guts to fire him, and Hollywood seemed like the perfect solution . . . I meant the perfect solution for me.

A real bad guy would give you nothing. A real good guy would take some interest in your career. He took a middle course. So he came to New York and he gave me two hundred and fifty thousand dollars to wash away the guilt of history.

He also gave him an object lesson: The money meant that if Jackie Mason was going to get into movies, he was going to have to do it himself.

CHAPTER SEVENTEEN

Jackie in Fast Forward

I didn't have a definite system when it came to raising money. I did figure out that a good place to start
was with people who had money. You have to be a
putz to ask poor people to back a movie. Nowadays,
they can't even afford to see a movie. One thing I
definitely found out — it always cost me five thousand dollars to put a deal together. That's the first
thing the lawyer would say — five thousand dollars.
Then he would start working. Naturally, they never
put together a deal, but I don't think there's a Jewish
lawyer in New York or Miami that doesn't have five
thousand dollars of my money to start a deal. All I
wound up with was tremendous intensity and a sick
drive.

Since I didn't know a lot of wealthy people, I started
to bother the kind of people that I felt might be connected with millionaires. I figured if somebody paid
a lot of taxes, I'd ask him about raising money for a
picture. If somebody was a stockbroker, I'd ask him.
And I found out one thing: all these millionaires were

all trying to meet me. As far as helping me, this was a whole other story.

But, I got started, as best I could, and I launched my career as a filmmaker.

Bobby Chartoff, rummaging through a trunk full of old scripts, offered Jackie a studio reject, a story about an odious informer who steals seventy-five hundred dollars from a Newark detective, then flees to Miami where he enjoys a brief, splashy spree. The con man falls in love with a plain, gullible secretary before he is tracked down by the detective. It is a gloomy story, dark and not very appealing. The hero is a loser. His girlfriend is a loser. Even the cop who tracks him down is a pretty sad case.

It would be a good plot for a Russian novel, but as far as a movie starring Jackie Mason, a performer most people associated with light comedy, it would be an uphill fight. The movie would be called The Stoolie. *The best you could say was that it was an improvement over the title of his show —* A Teaspoon Every Four Hours. *At least the title had some apparent connection to the story.*

Now Jackie had a script. He had a star. What he needed was money. After talking to the tax lawyers and the stock experts, after polling the family as well as all the amateur film auteurs he could find, Jackie estimated that he could deliver a finished film for half a million dollars. This was a low-budget minimum.

Of course, he was guessing. He had never made a movie before. He had no idea about how to run a production. No notion of accounting, no concept of cost controls or budgeting. The technical part, the actual machinery of it all, was over his head. That didn't bother him. Somehow, he would pull it off.

Not everyone agreed that he should take the chance.

"What do you need it for?" asked Gabe. "You're making a nice living as it is. What makes you think the movies are for you?"

It was impossible for Jackie to explain to the members of his family. Making a nice living wasn't enough. Being a local celebrity in the Catskills and Miami Beach wasn't enough. They were looking for a reasonable answer to a deeply mystical question. Jackie had to succeed because he required recognition on a vastly different stage from the one he stood upon as a stand-up comedian. He wanted endless applause, endless recognition. The truth is, he wanted what he could never have — his father's approval.

I don't know the answer. I know it has something to do with becoming the biggest star in the universe. I know it has something to do with my father. But exactly why, exactly how, I don't know. It's a mystery. All I knew was that I had the drive.

I went to a few different accounting firms and law firms in Miami to see if I could find out about such financial matters and raise the money for a picture and at that time, every single one said to me, "Money for a picture is no problem." First they would say we'll have lunch and talk about it. But they just wanted to show off to their friends that they're having lunch with Jackie Mason. Then they would start lying that there's no script, if there was a script they would think it over. Then they would tell me that we have to lunch with the guy's wife because his wife is his best friend and she's also brilliant about scripts, she's the one who first predicted that *Gone with the Wind* would be a hit. And the wife was going to help him determine if he should invest in this picture.

Then, after he used up the wife, he would try to get me to the bar mitzvah for his nephew because there's gonna be such important big investors at the bar mitzvah that they would put up the money for the picture in five minutes. I wasn't that stupid so I didn't go to the bar mitzvah so they would invite me to a dinner at his house with the family to try to impress a few families that he knows Jackie Mason personally.

This happened not once. A hundred times. And I would find myself not raising a quarter, but gaining weight. Gaining weight from lunches and dinners while they are desperately trying to impress their friends that they know me personally. Every time I went into their car, the guy has to make four stops to three friends and four relatives and shlep me out of the car because he has to pick up something, to get something. Right away, "Do you know Jackie Mason? This is Jackie Mason." These were the sickest people in the world and at the same time, I'm following them around, waiting for them to give me money for the picture. Then, if I put my foot down, all of a sudden, this same guy who said it was no problem getting the money says, Well, but my brother-in-law passed away and now I have to support his wife, my father is in the hospital and the hospital is in Africa and the trip alone is nine million dollars and the money I thought I would give you I never really had. My accountant robbed it, my sister took it, my brother burned it.

Then I would go to the next millionaire and the next millionaire. I was very naïve because I was desperate. When a man is desperate, he'll believe anything. Like a woman who gets screwed by three hundred guys who all tell her "I love you" and she keeps wondering why they all leave the next morning. "He told me he loved me." So, like this unfortunate woman, I would go on to the next millionaire. They weren't hard to find in Miami. I'd be sitting next to a guy in a cafeteria and I'd ask what business he was in. "I'm in the millinery business." What kind of firm do you have? "I have three thousand people working for me." They love to show off. I'd ask, would you like to invest in a picture? "Why not? What's the big deal? We have about a twenty-million-dollar business. It would be my pleasure."

The stock experts had a fee schedule. For ten thousand dollars, they would study the project and put together a proposal for a stock offering. For thirty thousand dollars, they would hire consultants and create a tax shelter. But they had to "structure" it professionally and that would take money. Up front. In the end, there were no tax shelters and there were no financing plans. The project was deemed too risky. Too far out on a limb. Jackie threw his money away on legal opinions and research fees. The legal bills had to be paid in advance, up front. The consulting fees were high and paid promptly. Jackie was busy every night working at the Miami nightclubs with their Naugahyde banquettes

and Formica tables, from the Attache to the Marco Polo
lounge, to pay for the legal opinions and consulting
reports that led nowhere. He worked three shows a
night, then broke his head trying to figure out some
way to raise the money.

Leon Charney, a lawyer who represented Jackie when
he was suing everyone, had a bright idea. He said that
since Jackie was uanble to find a willing angel, that the
best thing to do is to "go public."

"How do you go public?" I asked. He says, "You
write a prospectus, you give it to a stockbroker, one
who believes in Jackie Mason enough to raise half a
million dollars. I don't think you could raise a major
public issue, but you could get five, six hundred
thousand dollars." They call it a raggae. That's a minor public issue, up to six hundred thousand dollars.
I didn't understand the terminology and I didn't understand how it worked, but I realized that this is
the first time that I'm in a legitimate situation that is
actually gonna bring in the money because I met with
stockbrokers and we were all together in a meeting
and they were discussing how they were going to get
the money together. They didn't try to bring me to
dinner to meet the wife or to lunch to meet the friends
or to the nephew's bar mitzvah to meet the investors.

And I didn't have to put up any money because
they take it out of the money that comes in. That's
the main reason I saw that this was legitimate. They
took out twenty thousand dollars for all these expenses and I got four hundred and eighty thousand
dollars. Exactly how it comes in, I still don't know.
I got into trouble because the Securities and Ex-

change Commission found that this prospectus wasn't
a hundred-percent accurate when it came to listing
the assets. Well, lawyers like to exaggerate and they
could shade things a little to serve their purpose, because they said that I was going to do television shows,
too, and that certain cities had already bought it, and
that was only a vague wish. So certain investors
complained and the money had to be paid back, but
that was later. That was after. Now, I had the money
to make *The Stoolie*. That's all that I was interested in.

*It was JAMA stock, after JAckie MAson. Apart from
the four hundred and eighty thousand dollars he raised
in the public issue, Jackie used three hundred and fifty
thousand dollars of his own money. In the spring of
1971, Jackie was ready to begin. But he needed a director. He called a few name directors — Norman Jew-
ison, Sidney Lumet, four or five others. But they were
either uninterested or didn't return his calls.*

*Bobby Chartoff recommended a young guy who just
pulled off a minor success called* Joe. *He was on his
way to a big career as a movie director, but at the moment, he could use some work. The director's name
was John Avildsen, who would go on to win an Academy Award for* Rocky.

He would be worth a fortune in the future, but I
figured right now, I could get him cheap because I
am making a low-budget movie. I thought he would
work for four thousand dollars. He cost seventy-five
thousand dollars, which, at the time, was a lot of
money for a low-budget picture. You're not sup-

posed to spend a quarter of your budget on the director. But he already had half a hit — *Joe* — and I thought, Well, he must know what he's doing. I pay what he asks because I am desperate. This thing has gone far enough along so that I don't want to take a chance on losing it. I say to Avildsen, "You know, this is my big chance; I can't afford to screw this up." And he is very reassuring, telling me, Don't worry, this will make you a giant star.

The whole time I'm nauseous.

Jackie set up headquarters in an office building on 56th Street. He found that it was no big mystery, setting up a movie. There were associations and unions representing production managers; there were accounting firms specializing in motion pictures. The production manager hired the grips and crew. The hard part, for Jackie, was his impatience. It took two months to get the thing moving. There were casting and technical decisions. Jackie Mason had the title of executive producer. But it was Avildsen who controlled the flow of events. He picked the cameraman. He decided on locations. Jackie grew more and more nervous as he detected a difference in their pace and interests.

I saw that he had a very sharp eye and a very keen intelligence, but that this was no useful purpose in my life. He couldn't care less about why I was making a picture. I kept saying to him, "I'm making a picture so it can help my career," and he would say, "Are you kidding? It's gonna do everything in the world for you. You'll become a big star from this picture." I knew for a fact that he said this to a thousand people that he wanted to get to work in his pictures, that he just wanted to work and this was a pretty big budget compared to the budgets he was accustomed to and he had a good chance to make a big name for himself. If it served no purpose in my life, he couldn't care less.

But we got into the casting and the work and I offered the job of the cop to Art Carney and at the time he had done nothing in pictures and I told him that this was a great script with a lot of serious moments and since he was Irish and the part was written for an Irish cop it would be colorful contrast to me. I called him because he had seen me in the Palmer House in Chicago the year before and he told me how much he loved me and he said, "Oh, I'm interested, send me the script." A week later we got the script back from his agent who said he loved it but he didn't think he was right for the part.

Little conflicts broke out between Jackie and Avildsen. They were provoked by petty details, like the expense of the coffee, the style of the production. Jackie was goaded into a temper by his brothers and his friends, who didn't understand the battlefield waste on a movie set, whispering in his ear that Avildsen was squandering his money, telling him that the young director was making a shmuck out of him.

It wasn't only the money. Okay, it was a big part, but what really got to me was the fact that he started to get an attitude. Like I'm in the way. Like don't bother me. At first he was respectful, but it changed. He wanted twelve phones on the set. "Why can't we have two phones?" "It's better to have a lot of phones, we leave a lot of messages. Don't disturb me. We can't be penny-pinching about these things." My friends would tell me not to let him push me around, but I figured it's not that much money. I rationalized. So, a friend of mine or two or my sister-in-law Edythe would say to me, "Why should everybody be eating free lunches on you? In every business, people go out and pay for their own lunches. All day long, they're ordering, ordering, ordering." So, I said, "What the hell is this? Put a stop to this." And he would say, "Listen, everybody has to eat lunch." And I would say, "They don't." And we began to fight and battle and I said that maybe half need a free lunch, we could compromise. I thought nobody should get a free lunch. But, I was willing to bend. But the man had a different agenda. If he wanted a chair, he would get a three-thousand-dollar chair, the best chair in the neighborhood. I would say, "For eight dollars you could also buy a chair." So he compromised and bought a fifty-dollar chair.

Basically, I was insecure about arguing with him because a couple of times he made intimations that if he's gonna be disturbed, he's not gonna make this picture. So I would be scared because I saw this as a chance in a lifetime.

They began shooting in New York and New Jersey and then they moved down to Miami. Jackie thought that things would improve when they got to Florida. That was his turf. Avildsen would have to depend on him. But in Miami, Avildsen became more and more absorbed in the movie. More reckless in his demands.

222 · *Jackie, Oy!*

He dismissed Jackie's suggestions out of hand. He was the director. He outranked Jackie, who was merely the star.

Jackie, meanwhile, was too busy calculating every foot of film to act. His face, in every frame, seems to betray the fear that any minute he is going to run out of money. And all the time, the volcanic pressure built. Avildsen could look at it as a few weeks' work in Miami, but to Jackie Mason it was a wild, desperate gamble. All the years on the road, all the nights riding between hotels and bungalow colonies, all the shows up and down Collins Avenue on Miami Beach provided the blood money that Avildsen spilled so carelessly.

He started to get more and more arrogant and all of a sudden, I begin to see that he is reshooting scene after scene and everybody around me is telling me that this movie gonna cost me three million dollars. He is spending money like water. There is no excuse for shooting and reshooting. There was one scene on the roof of the Doral Hotel and it was costing a fortune. I said, "Listen, do you really need that scene?" And he would say, "Yes, I have to do that scene over." I could never win a point. I kept telling myself that I can't do anything about it and the picture is half over, about two-thirds, and the production manager tells me that this one scene is gonna be fifteen thousand dollars, but Avildsen says it's a very colorful scene, the most colorful scene in the movie.

Meanwhile, everybody is whispering in my ear that he's wasting my money, there's no reason he needs all this furniture, there's no reason he has to shoot it over and over. But, to him, it's never right enough. He was ordering three hundred chairs, five hundred tables, three hundred more workers and I saw that this guy is going berserk. So I finally got boiling mad and I blew up. "What kind of a shmuck am I?" It started to get to me. Something went into my head that I had been abused long enough. I blew my top. I became irrational. I walked off in the middle of the set and I said, "You fucking jerk-off, you're fired!"

I looked insane. I looked totally insane. It's like a guy wants to be quiet, he wants to tell you nicely what he thinks, and finally, when he can't control himself anymore, it doesn't come out rational. He was reshooting three, four times and then he called for a band and that did it. A band! Now he needs a band.

There was a dangerous streak of stubborn pride in Jackie Mason's life. He had very little patience when he felt himself thwarted. He preferred to try to exert his will by charm or wit or ferocity. In New Jersey when he felt under the tight constraint of a script, he stormed off the stage when he was in Enter Solly Gold. *Later, on Broadway, when his backer urged caution against opening prematurely, he bought back control of his own play,* A Teaspoon Every Four Hours, *and put it on anyway with the usual disastrous consequences. The pattern was always the same — he would plan and work toward a cherished goal, then, just before the climax, on the eve of the culmination, he would blow up his own work. Maybe he didn't want to know whether or not he would succeed. Or maybe the tendency was a relic of a child who was impotent against his father and therefore displayed a certain hot impatience with the rest of the world when they didn't pay attention to him.*

In any case, Jackie could not tolerate being ignored, being pushed away from center stage by Avildsen, and so he withdrew into his room and locked the door. Avildsen chased after him, arguing, cajoling, pleading. But Jackie would not answer the door. Avildsen lay down in the corridor of the hotel room and pleaded under the crack at the base of the door.

Assistants, henchmen, intermediaries all pounded on the door, sent telegrams, shouted that Avildsen would change, would stick to the budget. They all came. The production manager. The costume designer. But Jackie was unmovable.

Jackie hired another director of low-budget films and he finished the picture in a couple of weeks and the bitterness didn't end there. Avildsen eventually sued Jackie and won a fifty-thousand-dollar judgment.

The film, which started out with a budget of four hundred and fifty thousand dollars, wound up costing nine hundred thousand dollars, but the control remained in Jackie's hands.

It opened at the 68th Street Playhouse in New York City in May of 1974 and the reviews were respectable. Writing in the New York Post, *Archer Winsten praised Jackie's performance. "Jackie Mason plays this character, Roger Pittman, with that bottom-dog hopeless endurance that director John G. Avildsen seems able to handle with uncommon skill. It is a work of art."*

It may have been art, but it wasn't box office. After the first flush of triumph, Jackie began to panic. He didn't want a cult hit. He wanted an audience. There was another family council, ideas were batted back and forth — one brother said forget it, go back to the stage, another said be patient, the movie will find its audience, a third said nothing. Jackie went polling, he went to advertising agencies and tried to devise a campaign that would bring in an audience. Maybe a sexy girl in a bathing suit would bring in a crowd, although the connection between a sexy girl in a bathing suit and the movie he made was wisp thin.

The bathing suit sounded like a good idea. When I polled the public, I asked, "Do you think you would go to this movie if you saw this or if you saw that?" But it couldn't shake the image that it was a sad movie. Then I put in a fake campaign. I said, "Winner of the La Grande Film Festival, direct from Paris, in its New York opening!"

I figured maybe this would make it look like big art. Maybe art pictures will do big business and if it can't make money as a commercial success maybe it'll be an art film success. I knew nobody would challenge me on the award, festival or no festival. Who's gonna care? Who's gonna take the trouble to sue me for fraud? The La Grande Film Festival is gonna come to sue me for fraud? There is no La Grande Film Festival. Is the *New York Times* gonna send out a staff to look for the festival?

But the film died and it shows up on late television.

Now that I knew what I was doing, I was ready for my next picture.

CHAPTER EIGHTEEN

Jackie and Jyll

A few days before the Fourth of July weekend in 1974, the air conditioning in Jyll Rosenfeld's apartment building broke down and she decided to stand outside where there was a chance of a breeze while she waited for a friend. She picked a very dangerous spot to wait. On the ground floor of her apartment building on First Avenue and 63rd Street was a restaurant called My House. It was a coffee shop.

Jyll, who looked like a Jewish Gibson Girl with a kewpie-doll face, was a twenty-year-old princess who came out of the business end of a show-business family from Cincinnati. She had a weakness for cosmopolitan wit, and therefore was a sitting duck for Jackie Mason, as she stood outside a Manhattan coffee shop.

"Hello, how are you? Do you mind if I ask you a personal question? Are you married? You have a boyfriend?"

And then Jackie Mason kept walking, straight into the coffee shop to make a phone call. He left behind Jesse Vogel, an old friend who had a kind of Ichabod

Crane look, a lawyer, a late-night companion. Jesse was Jackie's rearguard mop-up crew.

"Do you know who that is?" asked Jesse, who remained outside talking to Jyll.

Jackie looked familiar, she said. She had a vague idea. She was, after all, third-generation show business. Her grandfather, William Bein, owned a few theaters in Cincinnati and her father, Richard Rosenfeld, was an independent distributor. So, although she was young, she knew a thing or two about talent and what's what.

Jesse told her that that was Jackie Mason, the famous comedian. He's a genius, but he's having trouble selling his movie.

I know all about selling movies, said Jyll.

Yeah, well, maybe you can help. He has this movie, it got great reviews, but he can't find an audience, explained Jesse.

Right, she said. Now she remembered. The Stoolie. Too dark. Too grim. You'd never know that the star of that movie was a comedian.

By now, Jackie had come out of the coffee shop, he had finished his phone calls, and he listened in as Jyll explained her own credentials. She thought the movie was being marketed wrong. She knew about marketing and promotion and even something (not a lot) about balancing books.

Her friend — the one she had been waiting for — was forgotten as Jackie and Jyll compared notes, took each other's measure. He detected in her a glint, a zany quality which would make for a perfect sidekick. She seemed like someone who would go along with any daffy scheme, and he looked like someone who could come up with some pretty daffy schemes. She would be a comic Zelda to his far-fetched Fitzgerald. He was funny, she was appreciative. He was needy, she was a provider. He was egocentric, she was worshipful.

But most of all, more than any other quality, she got it. He didn't have to explain the jokes.

"I'm a very shy person. I know it doesn't look like it, but I am really shy. I don't even like to tell an elevator operator what floor I want. I figure it's his elevator, I'll go where he wants. Maybe I'll get lucky. When I go to my doctor I don't like to bother him with my problems. He's a busy guy so I only tell him about the parts that don't hurt."

Which is how Jyll Rosenfeld became hopelessly entwined in the endlessly self-absorbed and compulsive world of a striving comedian: she stood in front of a coffee shop on First Avenue in New York City and got bowled over by Jackie Mason.

It wasn't long before she rolled up her sleeves and got involved in Jackie's business. She agreed with the ad agency guys who looked at the print ads and said, "Too gloomy." The first thing to do was to try to rescue The Stoolie, *pull it out of the dank hole where it languished, unobserved, in an art theater on Manhattan's 68th Street. Jackie was ready to try out the marketing ideas he had gotten from the advertising people to add spice to the picture. Jackie and Jyll went back to the ad agency people, they sat in meetings — two short, unstylish types — listening to the stream-of-consciousness opinions from the tall, stylish ad agency types. "Dark. Dark. Dark!" said the people who were said to have their fingers on the pulse of America. In other words, as Jackie and Jyll deciphered the marketing meaning of the incantation, "Dark! Dark! Dark!" — lighten it up. Jyll, Jackie's accomplice, noted:*

"Jackie gave a very sexy image to the picture. A different look. A girl with big boobs on the beach, since the main area where this was filmed was in Miami. A girl with big boobs would make the picture do business. That's what he thought. I wasn't so sure, but I thought it couldn't hurt.

"He reissued it and four-walled the house. That means he rented the whole theater. 'Winner of the La Grande Film Festival!' He opened two theaters in Brooklyn, two in Queens, one in Manhattan. One was on Main Street in the heart of the big department stores in Queens — a borough filled with Jews who spent summers in the mountains and winters in Miami and knew about Jackie Mason. We went there for the opening in a limousine and we stood outside the theater seeing how many people came out and as the people were coming out, we sent Jesse Vogel up to ask them, like he's a passerby, 'Would you recommend this picture to your friends?' They said that they were disappointed that Jackie didn't do a comedy. They expected Jackie to be in a comedy. For about a week, Jackie went through about one hundred and seventy-five thousand dollars and that was the end of that one."

Gradually, Jyll began to insinuate herself in Jackie's life, taking over more and more details of his career. By 1975, Jyll was running his career. Although she was young, she had a worldly way about her. Like all children of a broken home, Jyll had grown up fast. She had dabbled in her father's business, absorbed the talk at her grandfather's table, and knew about how money was made on movie distribution deals. She had also helped set up her mother's cosmetics business. But beyond that, she had an intuitive grasp of the business and the way that the world worked. She understood what unspoken items were not listed on the agenda. And she could be trusted. Her feelings for Jackie began as romantic, but she saw that such relationships came and went quickly in Jackie's life. She found that she had an affection for him that went deeper than sex or jealousy. She needed him like the father she never had. She accepted the other women. She accepted the unequal terms. She adored him and simply wanted to be around him. And so she made herself indispensable husbanding his money, attending to his appointments, reading his contracts.

Inevitably, there was envy and resentment from the people who had been handling his business affairs — his management, consisting of Bernie Weber, and his sister-in-law — but it was clear that Jyll had only Jackie's interests at heart and even more important, she had his confidence. He never paid her a salary. She took what she needed. He never worried that she would take more than she was entitled to. Once, she put twenty thousand dollars in emergency cash in his apartment safe. She put the combination to the safe in Jackie's pocket. Time and time again, Jackie tried to open it, but he never could. Even with the combination in his hand, he couldn't open it. Only Jyll could open the safe. Only she had the key to his apartment. It was fortunate for them both that they met when they did. She needed someone to care for and he needed care.

After the collapse of The Stoolie, *Jackie seemed to deflate. His usual optimistic buoyancy had been stuck with a pin.*

She started to talk to me about making another picture as that picture was dying, about raising money for the next picture and about trying to make me make a pilot for a television show and about how we should raise the money or where we should go, what approaches we should have about my career. My career! I didn't even know if I had such a thing. She got right into it, seeing if she could overcome my sub-star problem.

Some of my friends would say I was crazy to let a little girl run my career but I needed her. I was frustrated and anxious and very depressed. Everything that I tried went nowhere so I began to think, Maybe I shouldn't get too involved. Look where it's getting me when I make all the decisions, when I get the ideas. I was already twice defeated. I was tired and I didn't have the spirit to do everything by myself anymore. So when I saw someone like her was very involved, very intense and determined, I said, "Thank God somebody else is trying so hard. I can relax!"

And she was amazing, making forty calls in an hour to tax accountants and lawyers, to organizations and managers. She didn't get too involved in my club dates because she didn't think that this is her field. The Rapp Agency still handled my bookings. But right away, from the beginning, I let her try to take as much charge in every direction to see what she could accomplish. It's not like I had a big business and she took over. I had nothing going on and there was nothing to take over. It was just a lot of trying and calling.

She didn't have a title. I didn't have a production company so there was no title to give. I gave her the money. I wasn't the type of guy who cared about money; I never managed my own money before when I was with Chartoff or when I had Bernie Weber running my business. I was making money, working in Miami and in the Catskills, and she would tell me, "You should put it in this bank, it's gonna get this much interest." I said, "It's up to you." I was only half-listening, the money part didn't interest me. She says, "Do you mind if I take three hundred dollars?" I'd say, "Take five." I couldn't care less. And she took whatever she needed. She wasn't a gold digger that I thought would wipe me out but I was happy to help her out because she was limitlessly devoted and violently determined to accomplish anything necessary for my career. Her dedication was so total and she was so immersed in everything that I was grateful and happy to let her take over completely.

Jyll wanted to plunge in and make another low-budget movie, a comedy, to satisfy Jackie's fans. She would need a script, a director, a cast. But first she needed money to finance it.

As always, the threads of Jackie's projects and private life spliced and wove between his friends and family. He wanted to help his brothers and sisters and he also wanted to move along his career. Sometimes, the interests clashed. He was like a man who owned a factory in the garment center who employs his brother, his sister, his nephews on the grounds that blood is thicker than water, although not necessarily more competent. In Jackie's case, his siblings and in-laws were thicker than trees.

It happened that Jackie's younger sister, Gail, who paid for his singing lessons when he wanted to become a cantor, something Jackie would never forget and would always try to repay, was married to a nice, bright, religious man, Saul Schulman. Very orthodox. Very observant. But proved hopeless as a businessman. Saul was a salesman, a shopkeeper, and now he was in real estate. He was in on the contracting end.

In the blue-collar heart of Woodside, Queens, lay a dormant old building, Sunnyside Gardens, a beat-up old boxing arena in a has-been neighborhood.

At the start of 1976, Jyll had an idea for a show. An old burlesque-type revue with skits and blackouts brought up to date. This is what Jackie's fans wanted to see, she insisted. They would kill to see Jackie in such a show. There would be old-time slapstick comics for the purists and naked streakers for the prurient. The show would run for the entire month of May. Could not miss.

The one-story arena in Queens, where fans from all over New York came to watch the Saturday-night fights, looked like it had suffered too many losing bouts with the elements. The seats were torn up, the ceiling leaked, the walls had holes punched in them. It needed a major overhaul. "Can you fix it?" Jackie asked his brother-in-law Saul, a tall, thoughtful man, who looked the place over and nodded. Why not? We get in workers, we get in contractors. Bing! Before you know it, it's a theater.

Jackie gave his brother-in-law sixty thousand dollars toward refurbishing the seats and fixing the roof and patching the walls.

Well, that takes care of that! Jackie was like a president who thought once he issued an order, the problem was fixed. He turned his attention to the talent. This was his field of expertise.

Jackie enlisted Emile Griffith, a popular welterweight, to take part in the show, as a kind of salute to the boxing fans. He had "Looney" Lewis for the old burlesque fans. And lots of naked and half-naked ladies. They would run across the stage, imitating streakers. Could not miss.

Saul was going to book the acts and fix up the arena while Jackie went off on club dates to earn money.

Everything was set. He asked Saul when he came back from Atlantic City: "Everything set?"

Everything was not set. Saul had run out of money and Jackie was running out of time. Once, the fights at Sunnyside Gardens had taken place in a ring. Now they took place on the street as Jackie ranted and raved. "How could it not be finished? We have to open in May!" It was April.

"We have a problem: I ran out of money," explained Saul. "What should I do?"

Jackie went to a bank and borrowed fifteen thousand dollars to complete the renovation.

"Everything set?" asked Jackie a week later.

Not set. Saul didn't know how to book acts. Jackie booked the acts.

There was one other problem that Saul did not mention. The roof.

It was a hot spring season when the show opened. There were a lot of days in the high 80s. And the roof had been mended with tar. Tar suffers in the heat. Jackie didn't inquire about the roof. Saul was in charge. The walls were fixed. The seats looked good.

It rained off and on the day of the show. Jackie noticed that it was damp inside the theater during the final rehearsal, but he ascribed that to humidity. Sweat from the dancers. Nerves. He didn't think about it. On opening night, the theater was packed with an excited crowd. They all came in with umbrellas because of the rain and as they settled down to watch the show, they tucked their umbrellas underneath their seats. About ten minutes into the show, it began to rain. Jyll knew it was raining because it was also raining inside the theater. And not just a drop or two. Cats and dogs. Jackie looked up. Saul looked up. The audience looked up. The tar on the roof had melted, leaving gaping holes through which you could see the cloudburst. It was pouring on the audience, on the stage. The audience thought it was part of the show.

The actors and actresses were sliding across the stage in the puddles that formed on the floor that began to sag under the added weight of the rain.

The members of the audience were not caught completely off guard. Quietly, calmly, as if, this, too, was some choreographed part of the performance, they pulled out their umbrellas from under their seats, opened them up, and watched the show in the rain. While the actors ran through Sex-a-Poppin', *umbrellas were popping open in the audience. The crowd sat there like troopers, holding their umbrellas while the show slipped com-*

pletely out of control. The sound system failed. The streakers stumbled into each other. It was all done in triple time. Some of the actors even came out with umbrellas.

FIRST ACTOR: *"I want to be frank with you."*

SECOND ACTOR: *"You were Frank last night."*

And Jackie, trying to save it with his monologues: "Well, it looks like somebody forgot to shut a window. . . ."

At the intermission, Jackie was backstage, holding his brother-in-law by the throat. "You putz! You miserable idiot! Can't you do anything right?!"

"I forgot about the roof," explained Saul. "I thought my partners were checking it."

By the end of the evening, people were hitting each other with umbrellas, fighting to get out of the arena, screaming for their money back. Jyll heard the pandemonium and locked the cash box and hid on the floor of the box office.

Gail wept. Saul was mortified and Jackie lost fifty-five thousand dollars, but he didn't hold a grudge. This wasn't Saul's field. Jackie would set him and Gail up in their own real estate business. The main thing was to get on, to sink his money into something else.

I decided, listen, people want to see me in something that they can understand and identify with, they know me for a certain type of entertainer, I figured I'll do *Fiddler on the Roof.* As Tevye, I can't miss. I can sing, I know all the songs, It's my style of singing. There wasn't a Jew alive who doesn't know most of those songs by heart, and I spoke to directors and producers and I can't see how this can miss. I'll take this on the road and it'll be a gigantic smash hit.

On the road was Brooklyn. A high school audito-rium with nine hundred seats in a Jewish neighborhood so the people wouldn't have to spend a lot of money coming into Manhattan and parking. And in his usual manner, Jackie tried out the idea on everyone. Would you come to see Jackie Mason in Fiddler on the Roof *if it was playing in Brooklyn?*

"Absolutely."

Everyone agreed. People in coffee shops were almost unanimous. It was a brilliant idea. He took polls. He stopped people in the street. "Listen, mister, what do you think?"

Nobody heard a better idea that whole year. Could not miss!

They held rehearsals in a studio on Broadway and Jackie found that he could sing all the songs from the show, that he knew them by heart, and that he felt comfortable as Tevye. The people in Brooklyn were in for some surprise. He took out ads in the New York Post, *where people in Brooklyn were sure to see them. But when he checked with the box office, after a week or two, Jackie found that he had sold thirty-seven tickets.*

Meanwhile, all the actors are getting paid for re-hearsals; meanwhile, the director is getting paid, everybody's getting paid. We're moving in scenery and furniture and I am already out a fortune and we have not yet sold fifty tickets. These are cheap tickets — eight dollars and fifty cents apiece. Three days before the performance, I went into a state of shock. Immediately, I started to make conferences with all my friends and we decided to print ten thousand fliers and distribute them all around the neighborhood. This is Flatbush, my people, and they should be leaping at this opportunity. We put the fliers in stores, on lampposts. A mob of fliers. This is too fast, people don't know about it, but the fliers will fix it. We hired a bunch of kids and we had them going around and giving out the fliers. Every corner, every building, every door, a flier.

We sent a kid in every garage and put a flier on every windshield. We dropped the fliers from rooftops and we even hired a plane and had the fliers dropped from an airplane. And it was a bomb they dropped. Nobody was interested, nobody cared, we had eighty-two tickets sold for the first performance. On the day of the show, I decided to hell with it, I paid off the actors, I hired an act or two, not to disappoint everybody completely, and I announced that *Fiddler on the Roof* would not be shown because of problems with production. Instead, there's gonna be a variety show. On the day of the show we printed all new fliers, "There's gonna be a variety show tonight starring Jackie Mason" and a couple of hundred people came. I tore the house down, but nobody noticed. I lost about seventy thousand dollars and I was out of money again so I announced at the end of this show, "I'm giving back all the money."

Jackie's sister-in-law Edythe, who suspected that he might pull another stunt like that, took the cash box and hid before the show ended. The people came out looking for their money and found an empty box office. Edythe knew Jackie. He had gotten her a job with the Hy Einhorn Agency when she and Gabe were married. She didn't like staying home and being the rabbi's wife. On dates, Jackie took her along so that if he was not fond of that particular woman, Edythe could pull him away, claiming a press of business. She knew when to get lost, too. The relationship, however, was brittle. Jackie did not pay attention to business detail and some part of him thought that Edythe should be at home taking care of his brother and her two children, rather than working. Still, she was family and that made an enduring bond of loyalty.

Jackie could never resist the grand gesture. A few seasons back, he put on a show in the Catskills, Last of the Red Hot Lovers — *another wildly staged disaster. They couldn't give away the tickets. One day, Jackie and Jesse were taking the tickets to a ticket agent in Manhattan when they stopped at Yonkers Raceway. They watched a few races and forgot the bag of tickets. The next day, they were returned, untouched. He couldn't even lose them!*

Through all his own personal tribulations, stammering career starts and setbacks, Jackie was always passionate about American politics. Every day, he read the newspapers, front to back, and grumbled his complaints about the governor, the president, the mayor. In the summer of 1973, he was especially disturbed about the race for the mayoralty of New York City, which looked like it was going to go to an old-line political machine candidate, City Controller Abe Beame.

"*Ah, I could do better than him!*" announced Jackie.

"*You could,*" said Bernie Weber.

"*Of course!*" said Edythe.

These were the same people who would pronounce Sex-a-Poppin' and Fiddler on the Roof as brilliant ideas that could not possibly fail. Loyal, but shaky as far as judgment was concerned.

Jackie didn't just take their word. If he was going to go into politics, he wanted some scientific indicators that the public wanted him. So, he went out polling. He asked people in coffee shops and supermarkets if they thought that Jackie Mason, the comedian, would make a great mayor. Every single person thought that it was a sensational idea. Would they actually vote for Jackie Mason?

Why not?

And so Edythe and a small, loyal band of Jackie Mason enthusiasts — Bushee, Saul, Gail, all the nieces and nephews that he was putting through college and medical school — went out on the streets of New York City and began collecting signatures on petitions to have his name on the ballot.

Jackie, himself, did not appear on the streets until August. He was supposed to campaign, shake hands, spell out his program. But he noticed something when he stepped outdoors: "*It's too hot,*" he told the campaign staff. "*I'm going to the mountains. If they want to run me for mayor, they got to do it in the wintertime!*"

So much for his political career. Jackie was going to stick to show business.

CHAPTER NINETEEN

The Lyin' in Winter

After the collapse of his series of shows in 1976 and 1977, Jackie went into a kind of career hibernation. He and Jyll traveled back and forth to Miami and the Catskills for the seasonal work. He played the dates, appeared at the clubs, but it was a minimal state of professional life.

How was I going to save myself? How was I going to break free of this curse that was keeping me down? I didn't know which way to turn. But I thought, maybe, there's something I could do on television. I know that I used to go on Merv Griffin and I did something that nobody else did. I took questions from the audience. I would just go up in front of the audience and say, "I'll answer questions about anything."

People would say, "Why aren't you married?" And I would answer. "I'm too busy. You have to have a couple of days free to get married. Me? I'm booked up, thank God."

They'd ask, "Why don't you play football?"

"I would, but how would it look, a Jew catching a pig."

Merv always loved me. He saw me in Las Vegas and all during the late '60s and early '70s, he tried to get me on every show. Every day I would get a call from his booking agent to try to get me on the show because these segments were so popular. They acted like they couldn't live without me.

So, when the flops started and I had a little time between flops, I'd start thinking, maybe if I make my own television pilot, if that was a hit, that could be my answer.

The first place that I tried was Cincinnati. It was cheaper to produce there and the Yenta (Jyll) could get me a theater because her people were in show business there. So, I went to Cincinnati and I had guests and it was a sensation and then I tried to peddle it to the syndicators. Nobody was interested. Audiences laughed. Syndicators laughed their heads off when they watched it, but they weren't interested. They'd say, "Oh, we're very interested," but they couldn't care less. "I have to talk to my sales staff, I have to meet with my partner, I have to consult with my demographics" — I would always hear. But they wouldn't buy it. I heard whispers from middle-level people, the stage managers or the cameraman, "Regional," or "Urban," or "Ethnic." They would use different kinds of code words. "Too much New York."

A guy in Chicago tells me "People in the Midwest won't laugh."

So, I point out that the audience, which happens to be in the Midwest, is laughing.

"Yeah, one audience!"

Between the pilots and the movies and the club dates, Jackie's social life had a kind of surreal quality — something between Valentino and the Marx Brothers. On a not unusual Thursday evening after a show, he had his friend Morris Resner, a semiretired business-man and an old fan and friend from New Jersey, meet him outside the Carnegie Deli on Seventh Avenue in Manhattan. Also along would be Jesse Vogel, his law-yer and crony, in addition to his manager, Jyll. The three of them would stand there in the street, looking back and forth, stalling for time. Everyone was reluc-tant to go inside. Waiting were three different women — carefully placed at three different tables by Jesse and Morris — plus a man who wanted to start a business with Jackie's money and another comic who wanted to try out his act. First, Jackie sent in Jyll to study the situation.

"You got two in the back, two in the front, one in the middle," said Ben, the counterman. "They all got appointments."

Jyll nodded, calculated, surveyed, then came out and sent Jesse to a corner phone. He called the number of the deli and began splitting up the action.

"Listen, there's been slight alteration in plans," he told the first woman summoned to the phone. "Jackie has to meet a producer, then he'll pick you up at mid-night at the coffee shop on Madison Avenue. Make it twelve-thirty."

One down. Then the next woman was sent to a Chinese restaurant. That's two. The businessman was sent to an Italian restaurant. Jackie would be there in two hours. The last woman was sent home because Jackie had to attend to a family thing. Finally, having emptied out the deli, Jackie would sit with the comedian for an hour and relax. Until he missed the confusion and began piling up appointments again.

Jackie kept busy. His datebook was never empty. Always a young woman, between twenty-five and thirty. Always a fresh audience, someone who laughed easily. Jackie might grow more mature, but the audience remained the same, like a clock stuck at high noon.

If the mountains were a haven and New York was home, Miami Beach was an elusive temptress, teasing, enticing, seductive, but always unconquerable. There were lavish condominiums, colonies of Jewish millionaires — potential investors for his next project who paid lip service to Jackie Mason and his talent, who welcomed him at their table and in their homes, who praised him to the sky — but when it came time to put up the cash, they withdrew into their wealth. They might flash their boats and their limousines, but the fortunes remained chaste.

Meanwhile, Jackie felt the mounting pressure to make the next movie.

We had a script. The Yenta, Howard Loberfeld, a young producer and writer, and I wrote it. It was funny. It was called *A Stroke of Genius* and the story is about this brilliant scientist and the government is going to take samples of his sperm to create a superrace of geniuses. The Russians get wind of it and send this secret agent to get a batch of his sperm so that they can create their own superrace. I figured this would appeal to everyone — Russians, Americans, geniuses, and deli owners. I play the genius and I also play the part of a Brooklyn delicatessen owner, an identical twin to the genius, who comes to Miami Beach on a vacation and gets mixed up with the scientist.

We found out from the talent agency that we could get Karen Black to play my fiancée. She had a big name and she would be perfect in the part. But we didn't know how to get the money to make this movie.

The millionaires were all over Miami Beach that season. They traveled in great schools of limousines. Jackie said, one day, Listen, we should be able to hook at least one millionaire to finance this picture.

Fine, said Jyll, where?

Jackie had noticed that every day, at the Eden Roc Hotel, there was a high-stakes gin rummy game around the pool. The tables sagged under the huge weight of cash. Every table was surrounded with moguls and tycoons. No one less than a millionaire played in such a game.

"This is where we're going to find our millionaire," announced Jackie. "They love me."

So, on that Saturday afternoon, Jackie and Jyll dressed in their finest, most impressive Miami Beach duds. He wore his Italian blue blazer and Gucci loafers; she had on her Bill Blass ducks and blue halter. They looked as if they had just stepped off a two-hundred-foot yacht and had a couple of minutes to spare to catch a few rounds of a gin rummy game. They sauntered out of the lobby of the Eden Roc Hotel and down to the pool, desperately trying to look casual.

"Look calm," hissed Jackie, as Jyll's eyes traversed the deck like a search radar, picking out the real diamond pinky rings from the decoys.

"I'm calm! I'm calm!" she hissed back, not moving her lips.

"Then stop watching the diamonds!"

They stood smiling together near one of the biggest games — a prominent spot where Jackie couldn't be missed. He wondered if he looked prosperous, or if he looked like another second-rate flop out to steal a millionaire's money. He could see, every once in a while, a moving head stop in sudden recognition of a semi-celebrity. And by the pool of the lush hotel, Jackie and Jyll drank in the comforting smell of minks and ermines draped carelessly around the cabana chairs, baking in the winter sun. Not that you could wear a fur near a pool. But the guests liked to show them, to dress up their cabana chairs with an expensive coat.

Taking in all this untapped wealth, Jackie turned to Jyll and whispered hopefully, "They love me here, you'll see. We are gonna land a real millionaire tonight."

Jackie kept moving, always avoiding the sun, which he feared would burn him if he wasn't careful. He understood nothing about gin rummy, but he adopted an expression of high interest as he circled from table to table. Nobody stirred. No one noticed. These were highly intense players who wouldn't notice if the pool caught fire. They worked their way around the cabana and Jackie was getting depressed. "I don't think my strategy is working," he said.

Finally, from the direction of the lounge, a man approached. Not just an ordinary man. A blaze of light. He was dressed as no one else on the deck was dressed — a jacket that clung and flattered his lean, aristocratic form. A shirt with ruffles that bubbled out of the front like champagne. A winter tan that whispered money. Rings on his finger, caps on his teeth, and he approached with that wide open grin of a true fan. "Oh, oh, this guy's a big, big millionaire," whispered Jackie.

"Mr. Mason, I am your biggest fan," began the elegant man and Jackie leaned back on his heels, rocked and asked his usual question: "Thank God. Tell me, are you a millionaire?" The man looked confused. "I'm the maître d' at the pool lounge."

They didn't give up. Jackie worked his comedy act at the Konover, the Newport Lounge, the Deauville, and spent his evenings hanging around the expensive Jockey Club and the exclusive and private clubs — the Athletic Club, the Century Club — hoping to bump into his own personal millionaire.

All that it requires to make a movie is money. The rest, I firmly believe, falls into place. We had the script — *A Stroke of Genius*. I knew how to get a director and cameraman, how to set it up. All I needed was the financing.

Finally, I thought I found the man. A lawyer, and this lawyer said he had plenty of money so I was thrilled with the fact that he said he has all this money to burn. I wanted to be intelligent enough to question him to prove to myself I'm not being fooled again, but I was just proving it to myself, I wasn't really trying to find out if it's true. There's a difference between a girl saying, "Do you love me?" and the guy says, "I do." A normal person would try to find out if it's true. I convinced myself, but basically, I was just begging to be lied to because I wanted to hear that I'm getting started.

Now this man is a very prominent lawyer. A former state senator and he has a fancy office in a fancy office building and he takes me up there and he impresses me. I don't say to him, "Where's the money?" I say, "Are you sure you got the money?" And he says, "Yeah," and I said, "Close enough," because I was desperate. I would go back to my friends and I would say, "The man has the money," and they would say, "Where is it?" So I would go back to him and ask him, "You're a hundred-percent sure that you have the money?" He said, "What reason would I have to lie to you?"

Big, big man. Takes me to a friend's house. Three-million-dollar house. Fancy blonde wife who's over-done and overpainted and wears too many jewels. This is when Mondale is running against Reagan — 1984 — and these guys are major Democrats, heavy financial contributors to the party. And what am I talking about here? I'm not talking about a major investment. I'm talking eight, nine hundred thousand dollars. Looks like these guys carry that much around in their pockets.

It's two months before the start of the picture and I go to my lawyer again and he says, "Stop worrying. We're not talking about big money here. We'll put up the money in a second. Go start the picture. I got nothing to gain by lying to you."

So, the Yenta (Jyll) and me say, "He's right, what's he got to gain by lying to us? He's not asking for money." So we both calm down again and I'm laying out the money for the expenses. I'm signing contracts and committing myself. And when I ask, "Where's the money?" he says, "It's coming, it's coming, it's coming," and we got comfortable again and started with the picture. Now I'm investing in hiring actors and a director and it's a month before the picture. Where's the money? I started to become a little more sane. I say to Jyll, "Listen, I know you're desperate to please me and you're falling into shithouses with me every time. How many times are you gonna lead me into shithouses and I'll say perfect because you're taking care of business and you don't know what you're doing? Find out this time if he really has the money or not because there's something wrong here!"

So, this time she went to his office and she had a confrontation and she comes back, says, "Stop worrying, the money is there, it's gonna be there on the day we start principal photography. What has he got to gain by lying?" She had brought along an accountant and a lawyer from Hollywood and this accountant and the lawyer say the same thing. So again I feel perfect.

There were people who were trying to tell me something. I know this. Lenny Schindler, the guy who started the Famous Male Shop and was now running the Newport Hotel, he tried to tell me that something wasn't kosher. And some lawyer friends and some political friends. Hollis Batchelor (assistant

Florida executive secretary of the Screen Actor's Guild) tried to warn me. But I do not listen. I want this picture. I am breaking my back working in clubs, appearing in Atlantic City at Caesars Palace, signing over future earnings in order to pay for the initial costs. Meanwhile, a week before we're ready to start shooting the picture, this benefactor, this millionaire lawyer is still making excuses why he is not putting up the money. Okay, okay, he said on the day we start shooting principal photography, so I'll wait for that day. And on the day, Jyll calls and says, "Okay, we've started principal photography, where can we pick up the check?" He says, "Come to my office at six o'clock, you'll meet the investors and I'll give you the money." Fine.

At six o'clock, we go to the office. Me. The Yenta. Lenny Schindler. We get there and he takes us into a big conference room and in this room are twelve men all smoking big cigars and drinking coffee. The other "investors." My lawyer introduces me and everyone is pleased and honored to meet me and my principal investor asks me to sit down and I sit down. But all of a sudden, I am starting to get a very sick feeling in my stomach. Something is very wrong.

Jyll, I could see, is in shock. She knows what my stomach knows.

Lenny Schindler has this look on his face — he knows, too.

One of these men with the cigars leans across the table and he says something very disturbing, "Tell me, Mr. Mason, why should I put money in your picture?"

I couldn't believe this! I thought we're coming here to pick up a check. All of a sudden, we're on the grill!

These guys are sitting there with coffee and cake, having a party, because I know that this no good lowlife lawyer said to them, "Come on up to the office, you're gonna meet Jackie Mason. He wants to make a picture." They weren't there to invest in anything. They were there to meet me. This was a fake meeting. But I am in a panic because this has gone so far and I answer their questions. "What makes you think you know anything about making movies?" "What makes you think you're an actor?" And I say that I am knowledgeable and that I have already made a movie which was very well received by the critics and even won a big French award. Listen, what the hell, I'm here already, maybe somebody in this group will invest something. But I doubt it. I could see that they had a very cocky attitude — "You don't even have a distribution deal so you don't even know what you're doing!" They weren't going to give me a dime.

But, I wasn't busy and I made my whole pitch, nobody got too angry, we pretended that we weren't offended, but when I got that lawyer alone, I really blew up. "Let me ask you a question: Is this fair to tell us you got the money and that this is a meeting to come and pick up the money and it's only a meeting to try to convince everyone to invest?"

I really let him have it. He was very defensive.

"No, you're wrong," he says. "Something happened. One guy was definitely gonna back the whole thing, but he wound up in the hospital. Another guy got a sudden margin call. But two of these people will definitely put up some money."

But now I was back to being sane and I saw that apart from coffee and cake, this was a waste of time. I saw, in one terrible flash, that maybe I'll spend the rest of my life begging for money, unable to swallow coffee and cake.

The lawyer was trapped. First there was Jackie and Lenny, who looked unhappy. The lawyer wrote a check for forty thousand dollars, probably out of guilt. Or maybe it was the sight of Jyll holding a chair over her head, ready to throw it. But somehow, more instant financing was going to have to be arranged if the movie was still going to be made. Jackie mortgaged himself to the limit, borrowing from future club dates. He tried to get some money from Rodney Dangerfield's club on future earnings, but he was turned down. He called his brothers, but they didn't have a nickel. He called an old college friend, a guy who borrowed twenty-five thousand dollars from Jackie when his business was in trouble. But the old friend — now a wealthy manufac-turer — began to clear his throat and change the sub-ject. He called a financial consultant he had met, who promised to help whenever Jackie needed help. Jackie explained the problem and the man, who happened to be Irwin Schiff, a fiscal expert who traveled a thin line of respectability and would one day be murdered, said that he was flying down the next day to bail everyone out. He understood that payrolls hadn't been met, that Jyll was begging and borrowing, but swore that he would be there with the solution in his attaché case: thirty thousand dollars in cash. The next day, all work on the movie stopped as everyone awaited the arrival of their savior. The grips and production assistants — living hand-to-mouth — planted themselves in the office. Finally, Schiff arrived and in his hand he carried the promised attaché case. Not an eye failed to take notice. Jackie tried to introduce Schiff, but the cast and crew wanted to meet the attaché case. Finally, Schiff opened up the case and it was not unlike the moment when Geraldo Rivera opened Al Capone's cellar. Inside the case was one thousand dollars. Enough to pay the salaries of a couple of grips.

"Where's the money?" cried Jackie.

The frustration had become unbearable. They were always waiting for a vanishing investor. Always reassuring their creditors that the money is on the way. No one understood why Jyll rushed headlong into production. At one point, she had become so desperate that she actually said the reason they were hurrying was that they already hired the caterer. (Another disaster since the only edible food on the set was that of the vegetarians; guards had to be posted to keep the meat-eaters from stealing their food.) Jyll was too embarrassed to say that the backer had picked a firm date for issuing the check and everything else had to go by that schedule.

Now here was Schiff with a miserable one thousand dollars, which could not keep the production alive for an hour!

"I have something better than money," said Schiff, reaching into his attaché case and taking out a dozen copies of his new book on how to avoid paying taxes. "It's worth more than money."

The grips and production assistants — many of whom never paid taxes anyway — were not appeased.

Nothing stopped Jackie. He was determined to finish this picture. In his wild frustration, he lashed out at Jyll for her lack of care and caution — although they collaborated on every disaster. They wound up having screaming fights in the lobby of the Newport Hotel. She stormed off. He stormed off. But they always came back together. Their need was greater than their anger and, in the end, they both knew that Jackie was just blowing off steam.

I was on the phone all day long, borrowing, begging, pleading. At night I would search out everyone I knew or heard of and plead for money. I was like a crazy man, but I could not let this picture just die. A man from a delicatessen in New York, practically a stranger, sent me thirty-five thousand dollars. A stranger! Just like that. Most people were not so generous. A guy I went to school with, a guy I lent a lot of money to and who is a multimillionaire because of me, said he couldn't help me. He had nothing liquid! Nothing liquid!

I called Dangerfield's again, promised to sign over my future paychecks, but the club accountant said that he could not advance me anything, on Rodney's orders. Every day, someone was about to close down the picture and I was begging and borrowing and calling everyone I know.

Jyll, who was the director, although she had never directed a movie before, ran the eggshell production from the set, which was at the Eden Roc Hotel. The hotel donated twenty-two rooms in exchange for prominent mentions in the movie.

Every day, there was another crisis as another set of bills came due and there was nothing in the checking account to cover it. Karen Black showed up and behaved like a star, says Jyll: "She didn't like this room, she didn't like that room. Finally, she's riding in the car with me and Jackie and she says, 'I don't like the color of the light in my room. I prefer natural sunlight yellow.' So, without missing a beat, Jackie, who was fed up with her, says, 'So buy a yellow light for the lamp.' "

Finally, the Eden Roc needed the rooms they donated to the movie. A convention of doctors was moving in. Karen Black had one scene to complete and the use of one particular room was vital. Jyll refused to let the movie be stopped.

"I knocked on the door and on the other side of the threshold was this nice little doctor," she recalls. "I did this without the hotel's knowledge. I explained the situation to the doctor and he was very understanding. But he also had a problem. He had to deliver the keynote address at the medical convention and he had to study his speech.

"I said, 'Listen, we'll be very quiet. You won't even know we're here. It's just a small scene.'

"So, being a nice man, he agreed. That night, he is sitting in his room and there is a knock on the door. He opens it and there is Karen Black. Practically naked. 'Can I use your shower to get wet?' she asks, and runs past him. The scene calls for her to be wet, which is why she had to use the shower. The doctor is in shock.

"*Then there's another knock on the door. It's Jackie Mason. He is standing there completely naked except for an inner tube, which happens to fall down. 'Did a girl just come in here?' he asks. And he runs past this bewildered doctor who is just standing there with his mouth open holding a copy of his keynote address.*

"*The camera crew comes charging in after Jackie. The doctor, meanwhile, goes off in a corner and he falls back in his chair — still holding a copy of the speech while all these naked people are rushing in and out, screaming and yelling directions. Finally, they're almost set for the shot and I am standing near him and he says, in a very low voice, because he's from Kansas and very polite, 'You know, I'm not even going to tell the people back home about this. They won't believe it anyway.'* "

The money crunch was endless. Jyll calculated the exact day when all the checks would start bouncing. Including a partial payment of seventy-five hundred dollars to Karen Black. She convinced the hotel switchboard operators to shut down the phones. On that day, there was a sudden hush of calls and messages into the rooms and suites of the cast of Stroke of Genius. Everyone wondered what had happened to their outside lives, until the agents and managers descended on the hotel in person.

But every time it looked hopeless, something turned up.

One day, Jyll got a call from Jackie. Between takes, he was always out searching for cash.

"I'm here with a yenta who's gonna give us fifteen thousand dollars," he said.

"Thank God," said Jyll. "Now I can cover some of the payments and keep the set open. Put this yenta on, let me thank her."

"Hello?" said the voice on the other end. It sounded a little strained to Jyll.

"I just want to thank you from the bottom of my heart," said Jyll.

"You're welcome, dear, but, listen, I can't really talk right now. I just got a barium enema."

Jackie, it seemed, had heard from a mutual friend that the woman had some free cash, he showed up at her door, she said she couldn't discuss because she had to go to the hospital for "tests," and Jackie offered to drive her. While he was driving her to the hospital, he explained the plot of the movie. The doctor, who thought that Jackie was a close personal friend, let him stay with the woman while she wrote the check. The doctor refused to invest. The "barium enema" money kept them going until the next crisis.

There was only one time I felt really low. Like I'm a true failure. I went to see this Argentinian with a yarmulke. I was pleading and begging in the humble house of this old Jew. I didn't feel bad in the big office buildings with the lawyers. But here I felt bad. Here, I felt the desperation, I saw myself facing this deadline of closing down this picture. And I gave this man the whole sales pitch, how he won't lose his money, how it'll make him money, how I'll personally guarantee it and I'll give you a note to that effect. And he says, "I'll tell you the truth, I'm not lending it to you because I want to invest in a picture. I'm lending it to you because I'm a religious man and I know that you are from a religious family. I know that it's a problem for you, so I'll do you the favor."

That was the only time in the whole time I was in the industry that I felt completely, totally meaningless, a failure.

CHAPTER TWENTY

Still Crazy

A Stroke of Genius *was never released. It was, viewed in the clear light of the editing rooms, a hopeless collection of home movies. It just wasn't a film at all. When Jackie and an editor looked at the assembled bits of film, they realized that, no matter how cleverly they cut it, they did not have anything that could be put together into anything resembling a commercial motion picture. There was an unfocused, unprofessional quality to the material. Some scenes worked, others didn't, but all together, it was the product of an uncertain hand. Jyll was enthusiastic and bright, but she was not a director. "The common wisdom was that if you had four or five good laughs in a comedy, it would be a hit. We thought we had nine or ten and it would be a smash," she said. "We had nothing. It wasn't funny."*

And so it wound up, like so many of Jackie's schemes — both harebrained and sensible — parked on a shelf.

Jackie was like a scientist possessed, trying one experiment after another tirelessly until he discovered the secret formula for success. Jyll was his assistant, plunging ahead with him, completely reliable, if not quite completely surefooted when it came to execution. When she predicted that a movie would come along that would involve a mermaid and then Splash! *became a smash, Jackie was convinced of her good judgment. She also forecast movies like* Meatballs *and* Police Academy.

Through it all, Jackie kept up the club dates. He was a headliner at the Aladdin in Las Vegas and at the Concord in the Catskills and at the Newport in Miami Beach. The paydays were freshened by appearances in less-appetizing clubs. In Queens, he played the Lamplighter, a kind of cheaters' bar along Queens Boulevard — dark and desperate. But it paid the bills and kept Jackie's expensive comedy laboratory in business. But that wasn't all there was to it. Not just to pay the bills. Not just to keep his name alive.

There was the joy of performing. When Jackie stood before an audience, something happened on both sides of the footlights. People laughed, they always laughed. But over the years there seemed to come a deeper appreciation of what lay behind the humor. As if each laugh contained an affirmation — How true! How true! He took his audience back to a half-forgotten sound that reminded them of dead parents, a forgotten language, discarded values. They heard in his kaleidoscope of jokes a subtext of common sense.

And Jackie was rewarded. Standing there on the stage, he was not the object of contempt and scorn and ridicule he had been in his father's house. He was appreciated! He could actually hear, in the laughter and applause, acceptance.

"Let me tell you something; there's not a Jew in this world who can do anything with his hands. It's a well-known fact. And why? Because a Jew was raised never to use his hands to do anything but turn a page. To this day, a Jew can't fix a car. If a Jewish car breaks down, it's all over. He can't do nothing. Watch a Gentile car break down. In two seconds, he's under the car, on top of the car, it becomes an airplane. A Jewish car breaks down, you hear the same thing:

" 'It stopped.'

"And the wife says, 'It's your fault.'

"The husband has an answer: 'I know what it is. I know what it is. It's in the hood.'

"The yenta says, 'Where's the hood?'

" 'I don't remember.'

"Takes a Jew three hours to open a hood and when he finally gets it open he takes one look: 'Boy, is it busy under here!'

"But, listen, why should a Jew know about cars? It's not his field. A Jewish kid has to be an intellectual. You find any Jewish family, and their son's a truck driver, it's already a tragedy. A Gentile family, they're proud if their son drives a truck. They take out pictures of the truck. 'Look at this, my son drives this.' But a Jew is ashamed. You ask him what his son does, he says, 'He's in the trucking business.'

"In the trucking business? What does he do in the trucking business? Does he drive a truck?

" 'Drive a truck! My son!? Are you kidding? He doesn't exactly drive a truck. He controls a truck. How would it look, a truck moving by itself?

He controls it. He's a controller in the trucking business!' "

Over the years, as the Sullivan incident receded, he and his audience came to terms. They laughed at the routines and the pointed mention of his Jewishness without embarrassment. Maybe Jews didn't feel quite so vulnerable in the '80s. Maybe ethnic identity wasn't so threatening. In any case, the people at the clubs and hotels seemed to accept that what Jackie represented was not ethnocentric risk, but a man with a working knowledge of the oppressed. They were ready to forgive whatever did or didn't happen on "The Ed Sullivan Show."

Jackie was working Caesars Palace in Atlantic City, before the start of the Miami season in 1984. One night, he got a call from a friend at the Rascal House in Miami Beach. "Jake, do you know where your car is?" It could have been one of the urban commercials: "It's ten o'clock, do you know where your child is?"

The limousine was Jackie's child.

He thought that he knew where the kid was. In the parking lot downstairs — the car's bedroom. The driver was supposed to be available, at a moment's notice, waiting. Jackie kept close touch with his limousine. It was his one symbol of success, although the truth was that it was really a symbol of failure.

Jyll had wanted to lease the limousine for Jackie when things were bleak; she wanted to cheer him up. But they didn't have the money. However, Jackie had leased a Mercedes for her *because he wanted her to feel im-*

portant. Equity had built up on the leased Mercedes and Jyll used that money to rent the limousine.

Her strategy worked. It cheered Jackie up. When things got worse, when they were really in trouble trying to raise money for a movie, Jyll thought it would cheer Jackie up even more if he had a stretch limousine, with a bar and television in the back. But first she had to trade in her Mercedes for a bigger Mercedes, and then use the larger equity on the bigger Mercedes to lease the stretch limousine.

Jackie took an almost fierce, paternal interest in the cars. Whenever someone of questionable hygiene or habit — maybe someone with a cold — was along with Jackie for the evening he would send the limousine ahead and take a cab. "No smoking," he would announce to each fresh guest. "And no fat people." He didn't want the springs to be ruined. At that time, Bernie Weber weighed 298 pounds, and Jackie wouldn't tell him he had the limousine. But Bernie would see Jackie with the car and Jackie would have to make up stories to keep him out . . . like, "It's not my car. The studio sent it and they have strict rules who can ride in it" — whatever came to his mind. But Bernie would always see the car and one day challenged Jackie that he knew it was Jackie's. Jackie fumphered for only a second before telling him it was really Jyll's mother's car that she used whenever she came to New York from Cincinnati, and she had strict rules about who rode in it.

"But the license plate reads JMCO," Bernie protested. "Jackie Mason Company."

Jackie shook his head. "The JMCO stands for Jyll's Mother's Car."

So for the next seven years, Jackie's limousine became Jyll's Mother's Car.

Although when he forgot he told Bernie that the license plates stood for Jyll's Mother's Car, he told him that Jyll changed the license plates when her mother wasn't in New York to JMCO — Jackie Mason Company — to make him *feel important.*

Jackie rode around town like a king, although it was an impoverished kingdom. Sometimes, he didn't have next month's rent. But he had a limousine. The booking agents could see that. The hotel owners would see him pull up in his own limousine with his own driver. Jackie loved his limousines. The trouble came from the drivers.

The first thing that Jackie would do, whenever he got a new chauffeur, was to go out on a test run. Up and down the East River Drive. Seeing how they handled his machine. They could usually drive well enough, but Jackie seemed to attract eccentrics for the front seat. One driver brought along his wife when he took out the car. They were newlyweds and could not bear to be separated. This was all right. Admirable, even if it was a little presumptuous. The trouble came when Jackie left a dinner party early and came back and found husband and wife in conjugal bliss.

Another driver was a former New York City detective. Jackie thought that he was getting a bargain — a bodyguard and a driver. The former detective had his own notions about his job. He thought that he was an adviser. Whenever Jackie was in the car and deep in discussion with a guest about politics or show business, the former detective would half-turn and tell them that they were both full of shit. He — the driver — knew what he was talking about. Ex-police detectives can be opinionated.

The average rate of turnover was three weeks. One vanished with the car. Another, en route to Miami, got arrested in Virginia for speeding. He wasn't even supposed to leave yet. He was supposed to wait for Jackie. But, the driver got an early start and got arrested. "What do you want?" asked Jyll when he called from jail.

He wanted a lawyer and some money for bail. Jyll said no, she'd have to think about it. The next day the driver showed up at her room at the Doral Hotel. "Where's the car?" she asked.

"I left it for bail," he said.

"What makes you think we'd prefer to have you rather than the car?" she asked. "By the way, how did you get here?"

Then the driver explained that he flew. He wrote a bad check for an airline ticket. Could he please have the money to make the check good?

She made good the check and hired another driver. The problems with the chauffeur never stopped. So, when his friend called from Miami, Jackie suspected that maybe the limo might not be downstairs waiting, in Atlantic City.

"The limo's going up and down Collins Avenue," said the friend.

Jackie called Jyll, who was down in Miami, preparing the ground for Jackie's show. She ran out of the hotel and, sure enough, she spotted the car on Collins Avenue in Miami Beach, motioned and pulled the driver over. He shrugged and said he came down early. Jyll saw a corsage on the back seat of the limo and guessed what had been going on. The driver had been renting out Jackie's car as a prom-night limousine service. She fired him on the spot, but later that night, the limo was seen going up and down Collins Avenue as the driver fulfilled his last prom-night contracts.

Jackie thought that he needed a limousine. He thought that he needed all the symbols of status to keep his salary high. He earned ten, fifteen thousand a week as a minor star. But he could not see it leading anywhere. He was struggling and working hard and getting nowhere. He was fifty years old* and he could not see the breakthrough coming. It is a show-business truism that stars are always looking over their shoulders to see who is gaining on them. They are like the queen in the fairy tale who stares obsessively in the mirror and cannot bear the thought that there is someone fairer in the land. And when he looked out, Jackie always saw the stars, staring back at him in that peculiar show-business mirror — Mel Brooks, Larry Gelbart, Carl Reiner.

Jackie's father's curse — "Bum!" — sang in his ears. By most standards, he was a success. But by the standards of show business, where only superstardom is a success, he was a failure. With time running out, he knew that he had to succeed. To draw four, five hundred people a night was not enough to vindicate turning his back on his father.

He hit on another brilliant idea. If one comedian can get five hundred people on a Saturday night, and another can draw five hundred, the two of them should

---

* I always thought he looked younger (the co-author).

be able to get at least a thousand. Mathematically, it made sense.

Pat Cooper, the Italian comedian, was having the same kind of trouble with his career that I was having with mine. I always enjoyed his humor, talking about his Italian background and the frustration of trying to become a star, and I thought he was a very funny character. I thought that the contrast between a quiet Jew and an explosive Italian would be colorful on the stage and we decided to get together. We'd get out on the stage and he would make fun of my clothing. "Look at that jacket! Look at that shirt! Look at those pants!" And I would say, "Look at that mouth." It got big laughs It was an instantaneous smash hit. The first time we tried it, at Brooklyn College, a three-thousand-seater, we sold out the house. If I go in alone, I couldn't do half that business. Then we went to Westbury Music Fair and we not only sold out one show, we sold out four. We quadrupled our business. They seat three thousand people in Westbury, but you had Italians, Jews, and everybody else coming to see us. We would stand up there on the stage and attack each other, make fun of each other. He'd call me a short, neurotic Jew and I'd call him a loud Italian. The audiences loved it.

But the conflicts were real. We didn't get along so great because he was very intense and emotional and he would yell at me that I was late or that my suit was the wrong color or that he should come on first. He had this big thing about the dressing room. He'd say, "Listen, I don't care if I get the big dressing room, do you care?" I said, "No, it doesn't matter to me." Then we got into Westbury and he had the big dressing room, with the phone and the lounge, and I got a toilet. So he says, "I don't know how this happened, that I got the big dressing room, but listen, Jackie, feel free to use it anytime." So I invited all my friends and we went into his dressing room and we used his phone and it made him crazy.

Then, the thing that bothered him a lot, I wrote the screenplay for a movie called *Stiffs,* I put in a scene in which two people are making love on a water bed in a funeral parlor and the bed breaks and floods the house and the bodies go floating down the street. A very funny scene. It happens that Pat Cooper uses a water bed image in his act. Not identical. The bed doesn't break. He just tells about making love to his wife in a water bed. It's very funny but it's not comparable. He got very upset. He accused me of stealing his material. The situation got very tense.

He happens to be a wonderful guy and he's full of love in his heart and he gives money away like water to underdogs and hometown people who aren't making it — he's got a heart of gold — but something didn't work between us. You know how cold precious metal is.

The act lasted six months and then it fell apart because we had a difference of opinion about bookings. That was the surface reason. The real reason, I still don't quite understand.

It is always hard for a man accustomed to owning the stage to share it. It was especially hard for Jackie,

*who had definite ideas about pacing and timing and
how a joke should be worked. He didn't just tell a joke.
He rolled it out slowly, whereas Pat Cooper spat them
out quickly. You could almost see the impatience in
Cooper's face while the laconic Jackie toyed with the
timing.*

*And the clash of egos was not unexpected. Two co-
medians on the same stage, listening to see whose laughs
are bigger, like brothers watching to see who gets the
bigger slice of pie.*

But, there was an incident. . . .

All right, all right. There was an incident. Good
thing you reminded me. When I started making a
movie, *Stiffs,* which was another stiff that never got
released, by the way, he was very jealous. It was my
own production and Jyll had been putting it together
and I liked the story — about these three brothers
who inherit a funeral parlor, Alex Rocco, Jimmie
Walker, and me, an Italian, a black, and a Jew who
have never met before — I offered Pat Cooper a part.
One day, he just blows up. "Forget the picture," he
says. "I don't wanna be in a picture." Later, and it
took some time, he exploded and told me that I'm
doing a scene in the movie that is a direct steal from
his act. Something with a water bed. I was shocked.
He says, "I do a water bed in my act." So, I said,
"Can I make it a regular bed?" I'm kidding. It's not
funny. Not to him. He called my house and left a
vicious message on my machine, calling me a thief
and a liar. Those were some of the nicer words he
used. That was the end of me and Pat Cooper. We
died on a water bed. I felt very bad because I like

27027027027027027027027272702702727272722727272727272727270

him. He's a nice man. Lately we bump into each other a couple of times and we put on an act of civility. There's two false smiles between two fake people.

Jyll thought, Well, one great comic draws well, two draw better, let's put four acts on a bill and we'll own the town. So she rented out the Jackie Gleason Theater at the Konover Hotel and began advertising "FOUR big acts" every night. The Konover was an old swinger's hotel, in the days when Sinatra and the Rat Pack ran around Miami. But those days were gone and the Konover was shabby and beginning to show its age. It looked like an old hippie trying to stay young. The theater smelled bad, the walls were dirty, and the tables were starting to fall apart.

Still, there was a residual crowd of aging swingers who came to see the shows, and the best shows were still said to be at the Konover. Jyll began to sign stars to fill the blanks in the FOUR big acts. She signed Jerry Vale and Eartha Kitt and Jim Bailey and Debbie Reynolds, Tony Newley, Phyllis Diller, George Kirby, Allen and Rossi and the Andrews Sisters and Donald O'Connor and The Platters. She had filled up the stars.

Jyll wanted to do this right. She wanted this showcase to be perfect. As in everything else, it was all designed to call attention to Jackie. If the showcase succeeded, agents would come, producers, studios, publishers. . . . But it had to be perfect.

"I came down to Florida eight weeks before we were ready to open our extravaganza," said Jyll. "Four stars every night. I checked the room and it was good enough for singers, good enough for comedians. All the acts could play the Konover. They all had dressing rooms.

They all had accommodations. I even wanted the tickets to be perfect. I met with a printer and I decided that as long as we're going to charge a lot of money, we should have very classy-looking tickets. Jackie said, 'Perfect.' So we had white glossy tickets with four stars on them. Inside each star on the ticket was a person's name. No one could sneak in. If a ticket said Eartha Kitt and she wasn't there this week, we knew we had a phony ticket. Now, the printer drops off twenty-eight thousand tickets and we're putting them together and from the first week, it was a disaster. We saw that the system was not making money. At this point, we started to replace stars, to get cheaper stars, and so all season long, I was up in my room whiting out the names and writing in new stars. The printer was having a nervous breakdown. He was making stamps with the names of the new stars, so I said, good, make me an Eartha Kitt stamp, and we were stamping and whiting out and pretty soon the tickets looked like shit. Whatever we took in went to the printers."

There were, at the Konover, 325 choice seats in the section roped off for $37.50, although no more than seventy five of these seats were ever sold for a performance. The other 700 seats in the theater ran from twenty dollars in the rear to ten dollars in the balcony. But the people in the cheap seats invariably moved into the $37.50 seats and refused to budge. They all threatened to have a massive heart attack when security was called — riots seemed possible.

One of the first acts to be booked for a weekend special was Jim Bailey, who did impressions of Judy Garland and Barbara Streisand and Peggy Lee. Bailey was getting fifteen thousand dollars for a weekend —

the highest price of any act they had booked thus far. His road manager demanded that Bailey, who required a lot of heavy makeup for his act, be given a cool dressing room with a makeup fan to keep dry. He also wanted Bailey to be near the kitchen so that he could have a handy supply of hot tea to lubricate his voice. Jyll reported these demands to Jackie, who was already scheming about how to cut costs. His eyebrows rose. Air conditioning, huh? A must, huh? Good, let's turn on the heat.

Not only were the radiators sizzling, they put poor Jim Bailey as far from the kitchen as they could get. The man's face melted on stage and he grew hoarse, but he refused to quit. In fact, nobody wanted to quit. The Four Inkspots complained about the size of their dressing room, Jackie moved them to an even smaller room. But they didn't get mad. Marty Allen of Allen and Rossi had complaints. Donald O'Connor pulled Jackie aside and said he had smoothed it over with Marty Allen by telling the comedian that Jackie was having a hard time and to ignore the bad moods. Jackie wanted to kill the peacemaker. The show was losing twenty-five-thousand dollars a week and so Jackie decided to move to a smaller, cheaper theater — the Newport Hotel. When George Kirby arrived for his week, he was told by Jyll that the show was being moved to the Newport. Kirby said he was hired to play the Konover. Jyll said, "Good, you play the Konover, we'll be at the Newport." Unfortunately, Jerry Vale stepped in and smoothed it over. Another peacemaker! No one wanted to quit. On opening night, instead of four stars, they had nine people on stage: Jerry Vale, George Kirby, Jackie Mason, the Four Inkspots, Eddie Fisher, and Don

Phillips. There were almost as many people in the audience.

However, the switch of hotels did bring results: Anthony Newley and Phyllis Diller and Debbie Reynolds immediately canceled, which convinced Jackie that he should have put the show on in a sweatshop in the first place.

Eventually, they couldn't find four big names to stamp inside the stars. Jackie suggested putting Don Phillips's name inside a star. Jyll objected. Everyone knows he's our master of ceremonies, she said. How can you call him a star? Put in his name, insisted Jackie, but make it small. Put "from Las Vegas" big. Las Vegas became the star.

Then another group canceled and they had another blank star. Jackie said, put "Dinner in the Pub" in the other blank. So, it became Jackie, Eddie Fisher, Las Vegas, and Dinner in the Pub. Four Stars!

The brilliant idea landed flat, like so many of Jackie's brilliant ideas. Somewhere in the back of his mind, he was beginning to suspect that maybe it would never get better. Maybe he would be one more hungry comic who never rose above the category of almost-star. You could see them all around, sitting all day at the Rascal House complaining about this bad break and that disappointment. If only I had a good agent or an aggressive manager! Jackie always felt pity for such men.

But lately, at night, he had nightmare moments in which he saw himself alone at a table with no audience at all.

Eddie Fisher was a draw. He had a reputation for being unreliable, but people came to see him.

"*Our first show opened on January 15, 1985, at the Konover Hotel,*" *said Jyll.* "*Eddie Fisher came down to Florida and we never saw him. He checked into the hotel, went straight to his room, and never came out. He vanished. The only way we knew that he was alive was because we found food outside of his door. But nobody ever saw him. Donald O'Connor, who was in the show, wanted to meet him. Patty Andrews from the Andrews Sisters wanted to meet him. But he would not come out of his room. His agent in New York said that he was shy. He was literally scared of people.*"

Finally, on the day of the show, Eddie Fisher called down and left a message. He would not be able to make the show. He wasn't feeling well. The manager in New York forgot to mention that he was also a hypochondriac. Jyll went up to his room, talked her way in, and found him pale and thin and looking very frail. "*He said his arm hurts. I said, 'How does that affect your singing?' He said, 'It's nerve-racking.' *"

Jyll phoned the manager in New York. Should she call a doctor?

"*Oh, yes,*" *said the agent.* "*He loves doctors.*"

They also flew down his girlfriend to give him moral support. Eddie needed to have sex all the time. In his mind he couldn't function without sex three times a day. So Jackie's solution was to bring his girlfriend down. Still Eddie Fisher remained in his room. And now Jackie knew why.

I felt a warmth and sympathy for Eddie Fisher. Here was a man who came out of very sudden fame and success, who was as big as a star could be, and now he's working for five thousand dollars a week, which doesn't sound bad, unless you start to think about what he had been. A big, big star.

By March Jyll had moved out to Los Angeles. She had come to believe that when Jackie's moment came, it would be from the powerhouses on the West Coast. Florida was fading.

She insisted that Jackie make regular appearances in the comedy clubs — the Improv, the Comedy Store — where he would be seen and noticed by Neil Simon and Carl Reiner and Mel Brooks, the arbiters and taste-makers of American pop culture. Jackie was not quite so sanguine. He liked the East, but he saw the wisdom of what she said. You had to keep your name alive in California.

At one point, Jyll convinced Jackie that they should open up a restaurant in front of the Improv. They would invest sixty thousand dollars and have an excuse for coming back and forth to California. In addition, they would plant Jackie's flag in front of a big comedy stop, where he could appear when he was free. The restaurant was called Feed Your Face and, despite the name, made some money. But running a restaurant was a full-time job and Jackie and Jyll already had a full-time job: let's-make-Jackie-a-star.

Jackie appeared at the Improv and the Comedy Store, where the atmosphere was minimal and the humor raw. Young comics came down and tried out material, and the range of talent went up and down like a spike. But something was beginning to click for Jackie. He had come to a ripe moment of his life when he had found his audience. The jokes were now folklore. The routine

276 • *Jackie, Oy!*

*began to sound like uncommon wisdom. And there was
a sweet, self-deprecating quality to the style. The Jews
were no longer quite so touchy about their ethnic identity. And Jackie had grown older and more mellow.
The lines in his face were battle scars and the audience
knew it. They admired his perseverance, his sheer grit.
The hard edge to the political jokes — brash and
threatening in callow youth — could be forgiven in
someone older. When he began, after all, social unrest
was a middle-class nightmare. In the middle of his life-
long act, there were riots in the streets. The times had
settled down and his audience was ready to listen.*

*Jackie, too, made his compromises. The comedy was
not quite so bitter, so unforgiving. He and his audience
met halfway.*

"You take this Sylvester Stallone. Why is he such
a hit? In every picture he says, 'Duh-duh-do-do-duh.'
That's it. That's all you hear: 'Duh!' Everybody's
running around, 'What did he say?'

"Ninety million dollars — 'Duh-Duh, duh duh!'

"I talk perfect — can't make a living!

"People say he deserves so much money because
he's so handsome. Let me ask you: Is he really handsome? Take away his fancy hair, the way he's built,
and what have you got? Me!

"It just happens that I look ten times better than
him. I got a perfect body. His body is crooked. It's
wide on top, skinny on the bottom. It's unbalanced.
Who wants a person built like a triangle? You see
me? Straight. No mistakes. Perfect!"

CHAPTER TWENTY-ONE

Something Happened

In the winter of 1985, the late comedian Dick Shawn had put on a one-man show that drew a radically different appraisal from the critics. Shawn had always been considered bright, talented, but somehow he'd achieved only second billing, never great stardom. He'd never risen above small parts in small movies. The critics lumped him in with that whole pack of comedians who had come up against the marathon wall of the celebrity also-ran. When he appeared in the theater, however, the critics took a second look. Shawn was rewritten. Now he was "brilliant" and "inventive."

A bulb began to glow in Jyll Rosenfeld's head. Maybe the comics were presenting themselves badly. Maybe grubby saloons were not the best showcase for the work. Maybe the public was ready for the one-man show of Jackie Mason.

In April, she booked the four-hundred-seat Las Palmas Theater in a seedy part of Hollywood. Jackie was skeptical. He had failed in theaters before. He was afraid of one more head-to-head confrontation with a sorry *destiny. Besides, no one would come. The theater was in a miserable part of town. But Jyll argued that it didn't matter that the theater was in a rough section — it was a theater. That was the important thing. They wouldn't serve drinks while he was on stage. They would all be facing him, paying attention. Paying respect. Dignity came automatically in the theater.*

Then she did something truly brilliant. She dreamed up a title for the show: Jackie Mason's The World According to Me!

Suddenly, a bunch of lonely jokes had a theme. Jackie could ramble on, comment, do whatever shtick he liked, and it would fit into the all-inclusive framework of "The World According to Me!"

"Everyone is amazed at the unbelievable might of the Israeli army. It's a direct contradiction to the image of the Jew. It's an historical fact that Jews were never fighters. Jews were always pacifists. Why do you think you never saw a tough Jew in this country? You never do. I never saw four people walking down the street saying, 'Watch out, there's a Jew over there!' Let's be honest about it: Did you ever see anybody afraid to walk into a Jewish neighborhood because he might get killed by an accountant?

"In this country, Jews don't fight. I don't know if you noticed that. In this country they almost fight. Every Jew I know almost killed somebody. They'll all tell you, 'If he said one more word . . . he would've been dead today. I was ready. One more word!' What's the word? Nobody knows what that word is.

"Italians are just the opposite. Bang!

" 'What did he say?' "
" 'I don't know.' "

In the opening night audience were Carl Reiner and Mel Brooks; there were Larry Gelbart and George Burns, Alan Alda, Milton Berle, Bob Hope, Cary Grant, Jimmy Stewart, Jerry Lewis, and as Jackie went on, standing with a pointer before a map of the world, conjuring up the memory of Charlie Chaplin in The Great Dictator, *a great flood opened up. It was as if all the laughs that had been bottled up for thirty years were unleashed into the air of the Las Palmas Theater. The reviews were good — not great — but word of mouth began to build. Every night, Larry Gelbart was back. Every night, Milton Berle and Shecky Greene and Johnny Carson. Every night, they came back stage with tears in their eyes from laughing. And also saying they were sorry, as if they all had something to do with Jackie's long exile.*

Not that it was over. He was still fighting his way out. Every night. Polishing the routines. His voice deepening. His moves more graceful.

"You see, Gentiles do not know about food. This is not his field. Did you ever see a Gentile order breakfast? They only know one thing, 'Give me ham and eggs, that's good enough.'

"Did you ever hear a Jew order breakfast? Every Jew orders breakfast like this: 'I want it once over light on this egg and on the other egg I want it under a quarter. This'll be under a half and that'll be under a minute. I'd like a slight, two-minute egg on the side. I want the bacon, but not on the same plate. I want the potatoes on a third plate and the toast on a fourth plate. I want the coffee not to the top, closer to two-thirds, not less than half. I want the bread toasted, not very toasted, slightly toasted, not exactly toasted, but I want it brown. Not very brown, but it should look brown.'

"Gentiles are just as particular about the things that they know about. Do you think a Gentile buys just any gun? Guns are his field. He knows he wants a Magnum Two, Four, Thirty-seven."

It was amazing. He had never seen it like this before. Before, he had seen a half-empty house. Now there were no seats. Now there was a buzz in the air and you could think, if you were Jackie Mason and on the receiving end of all the compliments, that it was electricity. Night after night, the house was packed with celebrities. Something was going on. He didn't understand what it was, but it was terrifying. It was success.

One night, after the show, Nick Vanoff, a talented and far-sighted Broadway and television producer, came by and told Jyll that Jackie should move the show out of the Las Palmas Theater. "But it's a success," she said, not wanting to tamper with anything, afraid of breaking the spell.

"You should move it," he said.

They weren't ready. They were still shaky about it. Success, real success, was too new after all these years. They didn't trust it.

"Let's not make fun of the Italian people. The greatest people in the world are the Italian people. Maybe, God forbid, you're an Italian. All right, so we'll talk about something else. God bless the Italian people. My best friend is a guy, half-Italian, half-Jewish. If he can't buy it wholesale, he steals it.

"I got another friend, he's half-Polish and half-Jewish. He's a janitor, but he owns the building.

"I got another friend, he's half-German and half-Polish. Hates Jews, can't remember why. . . .

"There are a lot of people who hate ethnic jokes. And you want me to tell you the truth? I don't like ethnic jokes, either. Because I can't stand anybody who offends anybody. You should never tell ethnic jokes. Particularly about the Polish people. I'm sick and tired when people come up to me with Polish jokes. In fact, Polish people love me. A lot more would have seen my show but they couldn't find the theater. Did you hear about the Polish bookkeeper who was an embezzler? Ran away with the accounts payable! But, I can't stand Polish jokes. They make it sound like all Polish people are somehow dumb or stupid or idiots. I say it's nobody's business!"

After four months, with the success well-established, Jackie and Jyll decided to listen to Vanoff, who came by to see the show again and again. In September, with Vanoff's financing — because it took an eight-hundred-thousand-dollar commitment — they moved the show to Beverly Hills. The number of seats in the elegant Canon Theater remained the same, but the setting was bright and shiny and the gleam of good fortune began to settle over the show.

"This isn't the end," said Vanoff.

"I should hope not," replied Jackie.

"I want you on Broadway," said Vanoff.

And Jackie's heart sank. How could he tell Vanoff about the wounds he had suffered at the hands of the Broadway critics? How could he make him understand that he was seen as a Borscht Belt comedian invading the sacred stage which belonged to high art? Not to mention all the movies that collapsed under him, all the shows that he attempted to patch together — the accumulated disappointments of a lifetime bubbled to the surface with Vanoff's suggestion.

"I don't think it'll work," said Jackie.

"It'll work," insisted Vanoff.

"Listen," said Jackie, "when I was playing Dangerfield's, I got a hundred and fifty people on a good night. What makes you think that you are going to get two thousand people to come to the theater just because it's on the West Side instead of the East Side?"

"They'll come," said Vanoff.

The brothers looked pained when Jackie told them about it later. They had heard these dreams before. They had seen Jackie follow the piper to his doom time and again. "You're doing good," said Gabe. "Why take a chance? You got a nice theater, they love you, why bat your head against the wall?"

That's all he had to hear. Maybe the critics tore him apart when he opened with A Teaspoon Every Four Hours, *but he had learned some things since then. He was nervous. He was frightened. But he told Vanoff to go ahead anyway.*

"One thing," said Jyll.

Vanoff listened.

"You can't close us after two weeks. This show has to have a four-month guarantee. If it's a good show

and the critics murder us, we'll still have a chance with the public."

"You got it," said Vanoff.

And so Jackie came back to Broadway. In December, as he prepared for his Christmas opening, he walked through the Brooks Atkinson Theater on 46th Street. He walked up and down the aisles. He sat in the far balcony seats. He stood on the stage and tried out his voice. "Hello! Hello!" And then he went up to his dressing room.

"Would you like it painted?" asked the house manager.

"Maybe I won't be here long enough for the paint to dry," he replied. "Let's wait and see how I do."

There were preview shows for the critics and Jackie came out onto the stage to the music of "Masterpiece Theater." The spotlight kept vanishing and, trying to maintain his dignity, he kept chasing it. It was funny and symbolically pure.

"Hello! Hello! My name is Jackie Mason and I don't work with furniture. When you go to a furniture store do you expect to find a comedian? Look, I don't like to talk about the president, I'm not going to pick on him, don't get nervous. I don't make fun of him. God bless him. I think he's probably the greatest president that ever lived. That's right, and if not, who can tell? Ronald Reagan is a new type of president. This is why I don't make fun of him. This is the first president who doesn't get involved in politics. It's not his business. No matter what happens,

284 · *Jackie, Oy!*

it's not his field. He jumps on a horse, he eats jelly beans . . . a whole new type of president.

"Every president we ever had aged in the presidency. In a second, they looked nauseous and miserable. Carter looked tortured, agonized. Nixon's haggard. This guy just laughs.

" 'Ha! Ha! Ha!'

"You see, other presidents were always going crazy because they couldn't figure out the solution. This man doesn't know there's a problem. Problems are not his field.

" 'Ha! Ha! ha!' and he goes!

"This is the happiest president we ever had and I found out why he's so happy. He can't believe he got the job. Even when he does nothing, he looks so happy doing nothing you think he did it already. And everybody loves him. Because he does nothing better than anybody. That's his field.

" 'I'm doing nothing again.'

"Everybody says, 'That's it! Thank God!'

"He came back from the meeting in Reykjavik with Gorbachev. Remember that? He made an announcement: 'Nothing happened.'

"Everybody said, 'Thank God!' "

The show opened on December 20, 1986, and afterward, they all went to their ad agency's office to wait for the reviews — Gail and Evelyn in their furs, Joseph, Gabe, and Bernie in their tall black hats looking like stone-faced Indian chiefs waiting for the government to plant them on reservations. There had been too many such waits for this to be contemplated with pleasure.

"*We can always go back to Los Angeles,*" *said Jackie, who was eating a sandwich from the spread brought up from the Carnegie Deli. No one else could swallow. Jyll was on her third Valium.*

Nick Vanoff was outside waiting for the bulldog edition of the New York Times. *On Broadway, it was the only opinion that counted. The* Times *made and broke shows. The* Times *review was written by Richard Sheperd. Copies of the paper were passed around the room like poison pellets. Everyone in the room got one. They opened to the entertainment section like death.*

"*In his one-man show . . . Jackie Mason gives hilarious testimony to the art of the stand-up comic. He is such a deft comic that he is no less funny when he sits down. The giggles begin. . . .*"

And Jackie Mason sat down. For more than thirty years, he had been standing on stage after stage, suffering through ten thousand one-nighters, and now, suddenly, he had been blessed by the New York Times. "*He is very funny,*" *said the review.*

"*It was as if I had been blessed,*" *he would say later. "Before I was a nightclub comic. But you put a nightclub comic on a Broadway stage, it is as if you have put him in a beautiful and expensive frame. Now I am art.*"

Later, even the skeptics at the Times *would come around. Frank Rich, the chief reviewer, admitted that he did not like Jackie Mason and only came to see the show after he had been pulled and dragged by colleagues, after Jackie had won a Tony Award. "The show turned out to be exactly what I feared it would be: Borscht Belt comedy spooned out as if it were so much chicken fat at Sammy's Rumanian. Yet for all the familiarity of his attack, Mr. Mason was very, very funny."*

They all came around:

"In his Broadway offering, the comedian gets a few guffaws merely by placing his beleaguered-looking brisket of a body at center stage," wrote Newsweek's *Charles Leerhsen. "But Mason has no interest in these cheap, light laughs. 'The challenge for me,' he says, 'is to create the ultimate* tummel — *a constant body of laughter.' This he does. . . ."*

"When Mason lets his imagination fly out to the world at large, his comedy soars," wrote the New York Post.

Words were not enough. Every reviewer at the Times *had to make a pilgrimage. Walter Kerr, Malcolm MacPherson, Stephen Holden. It was as if they all felt that an apology was owed. And the Broadway establishment delivered its own form of recognition by awarding Jackie a special Tony for his show. The world was truly at his feet.*

The applause and the accolades were richer and more forthcoming than they had been in Los Angeles. The Times *"loved" him, the* Daily News *raved,* People *magazine profiled him. The new, hip* Spy *magazine proclaimed him authentic. He was tracked by the paparazzi and popped up almost daily in Liz Smith's column and the Page Six celebrity items. He appeared on Johnny Carson and was invited to take a seat without having to perform a monologue — an honored symbol of achievement. The lines at the box office never stopped. Publishers offered books. Producers offered leads in movies. Record companies offered deals.*

I don't understand it. It's basically the same stuff that I've been doing for thirty years. Nothing's changed. Maybe it's a little more structured, but essentially, it's the same.

Something had changed. He did not offend. He had paid his dues and he was welcomed back into the home. Audiences were surprised. They expected something a little vulgar. Compared to the shocking videos of Eddie Murphy or Richard Pryor or Buddy Hackett, Jackie Mason was mild. Even a little quaint. The accent had become charming. The audience was almost as delighted as Jackie Mason.

Why? I asked everyone. Why now? Why did it take so long? I couldn't get an answer. I don't even know if there is an answer.

Well, there is an answer — a Jew always assumes that every question has an answer, he's just not smart enough to know what it is. I couldn't figure it out. It made me crazy. To this day, I still go out and stop people in the street. "Excuse me, mister, do you happen to know why?"

Now that I am such a hit, every time I meet someone they tell me how much they always loved me. What I want to know is how come if all these people always loved me, why wasn't I a bigger hit sooner? Everyone wants to claim they were in on it from the beginning. But now that I am such a sensation I don't need them. Although wait a minute. I do need them because without them I wouldn't be such a senation. You know what I'm talking about? . . . Mister . . . ?

At the end of 1987, Rodney Dangerfield dropped out of the lead for Caddyshack II. *The part was offered to Jackie Mason. He closed up the theater for five months (he had bought the theater) and went down to Florida to star in the twenty-six-million-dollar film that Rodney Dangerfield quit. He basked in the luxury of the high-budget Warner Brothers movie. He had rooms in various hotels. He had his driver take him to the Rascal House where he showed his old friends, the ones who wouldn't back him when he needed it, what it looked like to be a major star. At the restaurants where he once dined in Miami Beach, he couldn't pick up a check.*

He had one bad moment in February when Rodney Dangerfield opened a two-week run on Broadway in his own one-man show. But the show was a bomb.

Reading the reviews in Miami in his own trailer, Jackie and Jyll looked at each other and said, "Thank God."

There were long waits between takes on the movie set. The other stars would drop in, say hello. Dyan Cannon, Jon Silverman, Robert Stack. His brothers and sisters flew down from New York and sat on the sidelines beaming.

It can be very boring. You sit here and you wait to be called and then you repeat the same line ten, twelve times. This is no way to make a living. On the other hand, it's not bad having a trailer and a nice hotel room and knowing that someone is going to pick up the checks, that they won't bounce. Very nice.

But I have a terrible nightmare. I come to the rabbis of Chelm and I pose to them this bewildering,

almost biblical parable. A man rises out of the ashes
of one terrible fiasco and becomes a great success.
He defeats all his enemies, he overcomes the guilt of
having spurned his father, and turning his back on
his faith and on his people, and is widely and uni-
versally celebrated. After many years of privation, he
has wealth and respect and recognition. And then he
is invited to appear on a coast-to-coast television
show and makes a complete ass of himself. He insults
his audience, he is not funny, he is a total disaster.
Tell me, what's going on here? Is this a punishment
from God?

The rabbis go into a huddle, and then they come
back and announce their findings. "We don't think
that this is a significant religious question."

I ask, "Is it some kind of professional death wish?"
They shake their heads. "Is this the father who has
come back and struck his son's tongue dry?"

No.

Well, what could it be?

The chief rabbi turns to me and says, "It could be
that he's a putz!"

*Ambiguity is the key to understanding Jackie's atti-
tude about his latest acclaim. It is embodied in a joke
he tells about the price of success: "When I was a failure, I wanted to become a star so that I could relax
and take it easy. But being a failure, I wasn't so busy.
I got up at noon, I looked at the paper, I ate a little
lunch. All of a sudden I'm a smash and they drag me
out of bed at five in the morning, they got me leaping
on horses, being dragged through the dirt, I get thrown
into the water and I don't even swim. How come I'm*

suffering more now than I was when I was a failure? This is success?"

There was one sobering moment that took place just before he left to film Caddyshack II. Jackie and Jyll had stopped off at a White Castle diner on Queens Boulevard in Woodside. It was crowded with lost souls waiting for some last connecting bus to oblivion. A sad, tattered couple sat huddled in a booth nursing cold containers of coffee. The man poked the woman and pointed. "That's Jackie Mason," he said.

"Nah," said the woman. Then she looked closer. "It's him!" she said. "You're right!"

"You think we got it bad," said the man, "it's a shame what's happened to him."